T0074579

Swarm Intelligence for Iris Recognition

Zaheera Zainal Abidin

Fakulti Teknologi Maklumat dan Komunikasi
Universiti Teknikal Malaysia Melaka, Malaysia

CRC Press
Taylor & Francis Group
Boca Raton   London   New York

CRC Press is an imprint of the
Taylor & Francis Group, an **informa** business

A SCIENCE PUBLISHERS BOOK

First edition published 2022
by CRC Press
6000 Broken Sound Parkway NW, Suite 300, Boca Raton, FL 33487-2742

and by CRC Press
2 Park Square, Milton Park, Abingdon, Oxon, OX14 4RN

© 2022 Taylor & Francis Group, LLC

CRC Press is an imprint of Taylor & Francis Group, LLC

ISBN: 978-0-367-62747-8 (hbk)
ISBN: 978-0-367-62750-8 (pbk)
ISBN: 978-1-003-11062-0 (ebk)

DOI: 10.1201/9781003110620

Typeset in Times New Roman
by Radiant Productions

Preface

Swarm Intelligence for Iris Recognition has been written to promote the use of artificial intelligence (AI) and swarm optimization methods in iris recognition. The artificial intelligence and swarm optimization method are important since they serve as great tools for learning, teaching, and research.

Iris recognition is one of the biometric methods used in an access control system. The pattern of the iris is authentic and contains different values of accuracy in the left or right eye of the same person, which motivates researchers and industry to use it as a template called bio-key. The human iris consists of spectacular colours and unique structures of a person to access the hardware or software applications or enter a building.

The application of iris recognition is rapidly evolved to fulfill the demand from its users. Early development of iris template was in binaries, which represented in zeros and ones that are called as IrisCode. However, the shape of the iris is not a circle but almost oval and not perfectly round. The size of the pupil contributes to the IrisCode to be falsely compared due to the flipping bits situation during the matching process, which turned bit '0' to '1' and vice versa. Moreover, a gradual change in pupil and iris shapes and sizes since the amount of light enters the eye, occlusions, disease, and aging are factors contribute to falsely acceptance result.

Therefore, the swarm intelligence inspires iris recognition to overcome the problem of false acceptance rate and false reject rate at the matching process. Swarm intelligence, artificial neural networks, and evolutionary algorithms have been the method of natural computing for making iris recognition in a better accuracy performance.

The objective of this book is to help graduate, undergraduate students, who are interested and provide comprehensive information about iris recognition.

This book consists of 6 chapters. Chapter 1 introduces the problem and contribution of iris recognition in biometrics. Chapter 2 presents the anatomy and functionalities of the human iris. Chapter 3 explains the first phase of the iris recognition system. The existing and current techniques in extraction are also studied. Chapter 4 gives the second phase of the iris recognition system. Chapter 5 explains swarm-based iris recognition. Chapter 6 concludes the story of swarm intelligence for the iris recognition book.

In completing the work on this book, the author would like to thank the Ministry of Higher Education or Kementerian Pendidikan Tinggi (KPT) for sponsor this research through the Fundamental Research Grant Scheme (FRGS) (Grant No: FRGS/1/2015/ICT04/FTMK/03/F00287). Thank you to CASIA and UBIRIS for sharing iris images. Appreciation to several people whose involvement has, directly and indirectly, contributed to its preparation. Thank you to the vice-chancellor of Universiti Teknikal Malaysia Melaka, Prof. Datuk Wira Dr. Raha Abdul Rahim, for her strong encouraging publication through book writing. Thank you to the dean of faculty, Prof. Dr. Rabiah Ahmad for the valuable comment. Appreciation to Prof. Dr. Mazani Manaf for his guidance and support. Special thanks to colleagues at Universiti Teknikal Malaysia Melaka who provided support and encouragement: Assoc. Prof. Dr. Abdul Samad Shibghatullah, Assoc. Prof. Dr. Zuraida Abal Abas, Ts. Ahmad Fadzli Nizam Abdul Rahman, Ts. Zakiah Ayop, Dr. Syarulnaziah Anawar, Dr. Nurul Azma Zakaria and Dr. Siti Azirah Asmai. Thank you to my beloved family: Zainal Abidin Abdul Hamid, Hapshah Md Dom, Zahri Zainal Abidin, Zahril Zainal Abidin and Zakri Zainal Abidin.

Zaheera Zainal Abidin

Acknowledgement

Thank you to Dr. Khairul Anwar, Akmal al Husainy, Umairah al Husna, and Zakeeyah al Husna. I appreciate your understanding. Thanks to colleagues for valuable comments and for making this book creation a reality.

Contents

List of Figures

CHAPTER 1

Introduction

For more than two decades, biometrics has been a reliable source of identification in access control systems. The application of biometric systems is seen in most system architectures, for example, smartphones, computer logins, building entries, airport security, forensic application systems and withdrawal of money from the automatic teller machines (ATMs). Biometric has been an alternative solution to password. Compared to other access control systems such as smartcard and RFID, biometric technology offers higher accuracy, security, efficiency, availability, uniqueness and superior performance. The biometric recognition system scans a person's body parts, extracts unique features and stores them in a secured database as a biometric template. Then, as the biometric template is invoked by a user during the enrolment process, the biometric system compares the stored biometric template inside the database with the recent biometric template and indicates a successful or unsuccessful match. If it is a successful matches, then, the system allows the user to gain access, else, the system denies access.

In the biometric system, there are two main types of identification measurements, which are the physical and behavioral characteristics. The physical characteristics consist of 1-D and 2-D, which images are scanned by the sensor that is static in motion, for instance, facial shape, face, fingerprint, vein, retina and iris recognition. On the other hand, the behavioral characteristics are human identification in dynamic motion, which is in 3-D or 4-D images obtained by the sensor such as handwriting, speech, voice, gait and motion recognition. Both physical and behavioral characteristics provide various modalities of human biometric templates for accurate measurements.

Even though various physical and behavioral characteristics are used for identification in the recognition systems, the iris biometrics template has been gaining attention from researchers (Abdul Matin, 2016), (Andersen-Hoppe, 2017), (Climent and Roberto A. Hexsel, 2012), (Tajouri, 2017), (Rapaka, 2018), (Ramya, 2016), (Sahu, 2016), (Ross, 2010). The iris recognition stands out as a promising method for obtaining automated, secure, reliable, fast and high accuracy for user identification which is typically 90% accurate with equal error rates of less than 10% (Daugman, 2016). Moreover, iris recognition is an autonomous system that uses complex mathematical pattern recognition, image processing and machine learning techniques for measuring the human iris (Daugman, 2015). Studies found that the micro characteristics in iris template have been mostly stable for recognition (Shen Feng, 2014), (Daugman, 2014), since the iris is an internal organ that viewed externally from the human body and gives a unique pattern, which provides a distinguishable template among different people (Bowyer et al., 2007). Nonetheless, the unique iris feature is sustained only for a certain time (Poonguzhali and Ezhilarasan, 2015), (Kevin Bowyer, 2015) and only for up to six years (Matey et al., 2013). In fact, the structure of iris template lasts only for 8 months (Konfeld, 1962).

Inside the human iris, there are many unique micro characteristics called blobs in iris template such as crypts, radial furrows, concentric furrows, collarette, freckles, pupil and pigment blotches, which distinguish the genuine characteristics of a person. Thus, the exclusive characteristics of a person make it suitable for iris recognition purposes. In fact, features of the iris shows the person's blood type, whether short sighted or not, aging, and health condition.

A continuous improvements of the new iris recognition with higher accuracy and efficiency performance are in demand since there are arising numbers of impostor user situations reported (Daugman, 2016).

In spite of the increasing number of impostor users in the biometric system, it is not a harmful situation and a major problem in iris recognition systems since the biometric template changed after a certain duration. The changes in biometric templates are due to aging, growth, health condition and clinical surgery due to cataract diseases that request the re-enrolment process to update the information in the database. Once the latest information about the biometric template is available in the database, then the verification process is easier, faster and less noise.

In the biometric recognition process, impostor users are categorized into two types. The first type (Type I) is an impostor user who is rejected by the biometric system as the genuine user who wants to access the system. In most applications, a genuine user is defined as the person who is officially permitted by the system owner to gain access to a certain secured system and have his or her biometric template captured and stored. However, the Type I user is affected due to the distortion to captured iris images and is categorized into two: (i) dynamic nature of iris characteristics, and (ii) occlusion. The dynamic nature of iris features is mainly due to health conditions, iris aging and emotions, which create instability in iris texture especially in the extraction phase. The colour of the iris texture changes due to inheritance and epigenetic diversity from different races. The constantly changing iris texture creates difficulties in the comparison phase to determine whether the captured iris data are from genuine users or not. Previous studies show that failure in the matching process was detected in 21% of intra-class comparisons cases, taken at both three and six-months intervals (Manjani et al., 2016).

Another category of distortion is occlusion such as eyelashes, cosmetic contact lenses, spectacles and hair. The occlusions affect some of the vital iris features which are not captured by sensors, thus contributing to the increasing noise rate. The iris template with a high noise rate meant that the iris images could not be captured accurately due to some physical obstructions (Rankin et al., 2013). If some of the information about the iris is not the same as in the database, the comparison process produces a "mismatch" condition and the biometric system rejects the genuine user.

In the meantime, the second type (Type II) is the impostor user who performs an attack on the biometric systems and pretends to be the original person. The attacks are concentrated to the biometric system points with different kinds of attacks for example fake biometric templates, spoofing the feature set, template tampering attack and masquerade attack.

The fake biometric is a kind of attack when the hacker gives a false biometric template to a sensor to gain access to the biometric system. For instance, a hacker using someone's approved fingerprint made from silicon and contact lens pre-printed with the iris features of the genuine user to access the building. The attacker copies the original iris template from the database and pastes it on A4 paper for accessing the premises.

Another attack performed on the biometric system is spoofing the feature set. Spoofing attack techniques attempt to deceive the iris recognition system by impersonating identities and increasing the risk of false acceptance or false rejection. The spoofing attack is performed at the point of the biometric device and system interactions using print attack, contact lens variation, sensor level and feature set level. Also, vulnerabilities of the iris recognition system motivate this type of attack to mimic the behaviour of the genuine user since the iris template is altered. For example, the appearance of the contact lens is not detected by the sensor and the attacker is permitted to access the system. The impact of the spoofing attack produces high changes misling commercial systems.

Template tampering attack is a malicious attack that changes the information of entire iris template into another format even though the watermarking technique has been applied. The reason for unsuccessful watermarking on iris template is due to an insecure channel between the sensor and processing module. The template tampering attack is targeted against the security of robust embedding that introduces distortions into the iris template.

The masquerade attack is a threat that is carried out during the matching process in the iris recognition system. This attack reconstructing the iris images to the original patterns produces dissimilarity bits in iris template. As the bits are not the same thus, the matching process creates unmatched condition and produces unsuccessful access to the biometric system.

Both types I and II are situations where the non-genuine user is not officially allowed to gain access to a system and does not have any biometric template captured. However, in either situation, the reason why the system behaves in such a condition is that when it detects what is commonly known as "iris with high noise rate", indicates a failure to match the scanned template with the stored biometrics identity. In the context of an iris recognition system, an iris with a high noise rate means that the information inside the iris image captured by the system is detected to be significantly different and cannot be matched for similarity with any of the original iris templates registered in the database.

Therefore, to reduce the noise rate in iris templates, techniques are used to overcome the high noise rate value, which is based on the elimination of the unwanted noise (Abikoye Oluwakem, 2014), (Vineet Kumar et al., 2015), enhanced the noise level (Gül and Kurnaz, 2016), white noise application and removal (Prajapati and Bodade, 2017), non-circular segmentation process (Noor Ajmed, 2018), (Yung-Hui Li, 2019), (Rachida Tobji, 2018), (Sun, 2012) and feature selection (Ying Chen, 2014). However, in the existing solutions, to a certain extent, to reduce or eliminate a noisy iris is still a problem. Among all proposed solutions, to solve this problem, the recommendation is to use only a certain unique part of the iris structure which remains unchanged for iris recognition. The unique part of the iris texture consists of crypts, furrows, collarette, pupil, freckles and blotches (Daugman, 2015).

To eliminate the unwanted noise, the shape of eyelashes and pupils are removed from the eye image. Moreover, the shape of human hair blocking the iris template is removed. Another approach for reducing noise rate is enhancing the noise level using the white noise technique. This technique increases the frequency level of noise. White noise application and removal eliminates the noise from the iris template since this approach acts as a glue paper that sticks to the iris image and captures the noise attributes. Then, the noise is removed from the image for better image performance.

Feature selection in the extraction phase is vital for choosing a subset of features of available unique features by eliminating unnecessary features since the information of iris features obtained can be tremendously huge and consequently consumes a lot of computational resources (Chen, 2014). In fact, in feature selection the features is searched and selected in the extraction phase. A current extraction method that finds blob features of the iris such as ordinal measures, is the Gaussian model of feature selection for iris recognition system. Nonetheless, the problem in the extraction approach is the lower accuracy compared with the standard value that is 99.99%. Furthermore, the detection of the blob of iris features is still under investigation.

The outcome of the extraction process produces 'iris codes' in binary image format for a compact data storage representation that is typically in 2 kilobytes. The small, light and simple binary image format of iris codes is important for iris data to be stored in the database. A binary image is a digital image that is represented in black and white pixel colours, which indicates values of '1' and '0'. The sequence of values of '1' and '0' presents the information of a human iris. Moreover, the purpose of the binary image is to assist in measuring the distance of pixels efficiently and is also found to be useful for the next matching process.

However, the existing matching approaches are incapable of identifying the changes in iris texture like having high FRR rates although the person is a genuine user. Therefore, the problem of 'failure-to-match' occurs between the real iris template and the stored one due to the lack of a natural computational algorithm in estimating the changes in the iris texture. On the other hand, the iris features change as the person has a disease, aging, growth and emotional instability. Another problem existing in the matching phase is the 'flipping-bits' situation, in which several '1' is flipped to be '0' and vice versa inside the 2 kilobyte iris template. Thus, the 'flipping-bits' problem creates a volatile environment that creates a difficult situation for the matching process.

The need for unique blob features identification is important to reduce the failure-to-match problem. Moreover, blob matching is based on binary representation, which created a flipping bits situation that made the unique iris features different from the database and difficult for the comparison phase. The current method of matching using Hamming Distance for comparison is being used to solve this problem.

It has been found that the most authentic and unique iris features reduce the equal error rate (EER) from a high noise iris. If the error rate is reduced, higher accuracy performance can be achieved. It contains information on the iris in terms of equal error rates. Errors are important to measure the accuracy of iris recognition. Errors determine whether the system should reject or accept the original user. The accuracy parameter is determined as false rejection error (FRR) (type I error), which occurs when a system falsely rejects a genuine user and acknowledges the impostor. A false acceptance error (FAR) (type II error) occurs when a system falsely identifies an impostor as a genuine user. The intersection points between the FRR and FAR are called the equal error rate (EER), which is used to measure the accuracy of the biometric systems. A lower EER indicates higher accuracy in the biometric systems. Threshold means the filter that eliminates the biometric reference identifier associated with biometric reference and the identifier for a biometric probe that has not successfully attained a level of any type of matching score.

The performance criteria mean the proposed approach is self-searching the changes in iris texture, and self-learn in selecting the authentic iris features, and self-comparing against the unique features of iris texture. Moreover, the new approach produces higher accuracy performance in its benchmark. On the other hand, it gives faster identification for iris recognition.

Based on the industry perspective, high noise rates in iris template issues produce several assumptions whether the biometric system is suitable for extracting unique features to determine the genuine user, able to self-learn in searching for unique features of the image in the matching phase and the new approach recognize unique iris features (crypt and radial furrow) in iris recognition.

Therefore, the unique iris feature selected is based on the best feature points from the entire iris texture, which is required in learning the changes or instability in iris texture intelligently and naturally. The natural computational algorithms consist of artificial neural networks, artificial immune systems, evolutionary algorithms, and swarm intelligence.

An artificial neural network (ANN) is the component of artificial intelligence that is meant to simulate the functioning of a human brain. Processing units make up ANNs, which in turn consist of inputs and outputs. The inputs determine a way for the ANN learns to produce the desired output called neural networks, or connectionist systems which are computing systems vaguely inspired by the biological neural networks that constitute animal brains. The data structures and functionality of neural nets are designed to simulate associative memory.

The advantages of ANN in iris recognition are the neural networks used to detect iris colour and iris images from both eyes simultaneously tested for the comparison process. The process provided an increased accuracy and performance when applied on CASIA Iris database V3 providing a false positive and false negative rate of 0% and 9.96% respectively while the overall accuracy was 99.92%.

The disadvantages of ANN in iris recognition are that the iris feature vectors are fed to a backpropagation neural network having one hidden layer of 10 neurons. Increasing the number of neurons in the hidden layer was investigated and found a recognition rate low in percentage that is 75% and a low improvement to the achieved recognition rate.

The artificial immune systems are crucial for data analysis and consist of a set of B cells, links between those B cells (used to support the B cell in the network via its stimulation level) and cloning and mutation operations that are performed on the B cell objects. In the real immune system, pathogens produce antigens when invading a host. It is these antigens that are matched with the antibodies of the immune system. For the sake of simplicity in the AIS separate antigens are not created, the complete data items are considered to be representative of antigens rather than entire pathogens (Jon Timmis, 2000).

Advantages of AIS are it can clone itself for learning and is capable of responding to a stimulus closely matching that data item (analogous to the real immune system where B cells respond to particular antigens). Stimulus relates both to how well its antibody binds to the antigen and to its affinity (or enmity) to its neighbours in the network (Farmer et al., 1986). The cells which remain specific to the original invader are retained within the body and contribute to the immunological memory specific to that particular antigen. Those cells which vary in some way from their parent cell allow the immune system to adapt to variations in the antigen (due to for example a mutation in the infecting agent). This allows the immune system to 'pre-empt' further infections. In the same way, the AIS clones and mutates B cells to build up a memory of B cells that can identify similar patterns to the one that caused the cloning. This process allows areas of similarity to emerge as clusters of cells in the network that identify certain types of data patterns. It is important to note that only those cells which are sufficiently closely related to active parts of the network survive.

The evolutionary algorithm is applying the memetic algorithm and genetic algorithm that finds the circle of external iris and pupil border in an edge map. In the iris segmentation process, it starts with localization of the region in an eye, normalization of the region, feature encoding and matching. Canny edge detection is used to transform a grey-scaled eye image into the binary edge map, which contains the imaginary circle and edge pixels.

The good thing about the evolutionary algorithm is it performed better than Circular Hough Transform and higher inaccuracy. However, the iris template changes in slow motion, so demand for a new algorithm using natural computing languages to naturally learn the iris template is high, since the iris template keeps changing and a new method needs to be produced that finds the iris feature in a natural way. Natural computing helps iris recognition such as artificial intelligence, fuzzy, genetic algorithm and swarm intelligence.

In swarm intelligence, particle swarm optimization (PSO) and ant colony optimization (ACO) is the most used nature-inspired algorithms to solve optimization problems in iris recognition. Swarm algorithms are chosen based on their winning criteria. Two of the most prominent criteria that make them preferred algorithms are they search the element using stigmergy mechanism and achieve faster computational time compared with other nature inspired computational algorithms.

ACO is used to select the best iris feature from the iris texture. The advantages of ACO compared to PSO are; it intelligently handles noise better than PSO, which gives a good PSNR value, accurate detection of unique features in iris recognition, and faster encoding time (Zhu, 2019).

However, the disadvantage of ACO takes a longer time in iteration to converge in arriving at optimal solutions due to random movements of the artificial ants. To stop the iteration of movement, a target needs to be initialized for an ant to start searching for the unique iris features and end the process after meeting the target value. This fusion method has been combined with Content based Image Retrieval field to develop a new approach.

A new approach named as modified ant colony optimization selects the most important unique iris features which naturally adapt to the changes in the iris characteristics. The unique features of crypts and radial furrows were chosen based on literature evidence in (Neelima Chintala, 2017) and (Zaheera, 2014). Most studies also stated that these two features are the most stable iris features for a certain duration of time. The artificial ant finds the best crypts and radial furrows based on the region of interest on stigmergy analogy, the number of pheromones and the movement of ants forward and backward that finally determine the optimum solution. The optimal solution represents the iris features model for identification and extraction to be used during verification processes. The comparison is made through the pattern of the iris texture in the confusion matrix and image-based comparison that is directly evaluated between the iris feature image and the stored iris image in the database.

The new approach of crypt and furrow detection in iris features is using modified ant colony optimization. Crypt and furrow are detected during the extraction phase and then stored in indexed images. The outcome of this new approach is to reduce the Equal Error Rate and establish confirmation whether a user is genuine or non-genuine. To achieve the aim of this book, implementation of objectives has enhanced the new model of iris extraction using ant colony optimization and content-based image retrieval (modified ant colony optimization), constructed the new approach of image-based matching for iris recognition and proposed the new approach for iris recognition based on unique iris features (crypt and radial furrow) using modified ant colony optimization.

The scope covers the first and second generation of iris recognition in biometric systems. The iris is among the physiological traits which is understudied, after fingerprints, and facial features. Generally, the iris is located in between the pupil and sclera in an eye which consists of pupillary and ciliary zones. The pupillary zone contains the pupil frills and collarette, which help in pupil shrinkage and expand. On the other hand, the cillary zone covers micro features in the iris for example, furrows, crypts, rings, freckles, and pigment blotches that determine the authenticity of a person. The cilliary zone provides more micro features compared to the pupillary zone and unique to every person. Furthermore, the iris is a muscle that controls the amount of light entering an eye which has variations of contraction and dilation movements. However, variations in iris occurs due to numerous factors for instance, pupil dilation, distorted iris and occlusion. The pupil dilation means changes in diameter and radius of the almost circular pupil shape due to the contraction of the iris muscle, which is caused by the amount of light entering the eye. Besides, iris distortion happens when a person has an eye disease, eye surgery (i.e., cataract) and low condition of health (i.e., fever). Nevertheless, pupil dilation is out of scope to measure the variations, since it takes longer time durations to complete the movement.

Although techniques have been done to overcome issues in iris distortion and occlusions however, iris recognition systems are still facing challenges to determine blob features inside the iris. Therefore, in this book, the proposed approach shall focus on detecting only certain blob features inside the iris texture which are crypts and furrows. In order to obtain iris images, the public databases of the eye images were downloaded from CASIA and UBIRIS for further investigation. The eye images were in the format of (.bmp), (.png) and (.jpg).

Early iris recognition system compare IrisCode in binary format. Integral Daugman Operator (IDO) and Hough Transform (HT) generated the segmented and normalized iris in circular shape. However, the shape of the iris is not a circle but almost oval and not perfectly round. In fact, the size of the pupil contributes to the IrisCode to be falsely compared due to a flipping bits situation during the matching process. The flipping bits condition turns bit '0' to '1' and vice versa since a gradual change in pupil and iris shape and size due to the amount of light entering the eye, occlusions, diseases and aging.

Therefore, the idea of the non-circular method is introduced to assist the iris recognition system to obtain a successful matching process. Along the journey, researchers found that a computer needs to learn human behaviour and characteristics according to human specifications that request a technique for it to mimic human behaviour in order for it to act like a human. Thus, artificial intelligence came into the picture. Swarm intelligence, artificial neural networks and evolutionary algorithms have been the method of natural computing algorithms that falls under the artificial intelligence (AI) category for making iris recognition perform more accurately.

Chapter 2 describes about the structure and functionalities of the human iris. Chapter 3 explains the first generation of iris recognition systems. Chapter 4 gives the second generation of iris recognition systems. Chapter 5 explains swarm-based iris recognition. Chapter 6 concludes the story of swarm intelligence for iris recognition.

Human Eye

Chapter 2 explains the anatomy of the human eye. The eye contains various complex components that have their functions. From the many parts of the eye, the iris has been studied for recognition in biometric systems due to high performance accuracy. Biologically, the iris is a layer of muscles that control the amount of light entering the eye. However, from another perspective, it is seen as a "key" to access the digital world due to its unique features and authenticity.

2.1 OVERVIEW

Every human has a pair of remarkable and amazing eyes. The eye is an internal organ in a human body that is seen from the outside. The human eye consists of complex parts such as the lens, retina, cornea, pupil and iris. The lens is a near transparent biconvex structure that is located at the back of the iris. It assists in focussing light rays onto the retina for a human to view objects from a distance or zooming on tiny objects from a closer distance. The lens is developed from unusually elongated cells that get nutrients from surrounding fluids, which is the aqueous humour. The shape of the lens can be adjusted according to the contraction and dilation of the ciliary muscles thus allowing the eye to view clearly at varied distances.

The retina is a transparent tissue comprising several layers and sensitive to light. It helps to translate the image into electrical neural impulses to the brain to create visual perception. When light enters the eye, it permits focusing an image onto the retina through the cornea and lens. The molecules in the rods and cones react to wavelengths of light and trigger nerve impulses. These impulses are turned into a pattern in the retina cell layers and carried through the optic nerve to visual centres of the brain, for image interpretation.

Besides, the cornea is the transparent layer in front of the eye that always remains moist. The purpose of the cornea is to protect the iris and the pupil from danger. The cornea provides a better focusing system for the eye, which consists of plenty of nerves and it inverts the image onto the retina. Nonetheless, as human ages, the cornea becomes less dome shaped and the focusing power decreases. Figure 1 shows the anatomy of the human eye. The pupil is a hole located in the centre of the iris that allows light to enter the eye through the lens and hits the retina. The pupil appears to be black due to the light that has been absorbed by the surrounding tissues inside the eye.

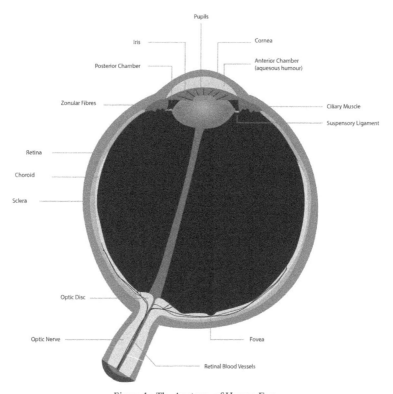

Figure 1: The Anatomy of Human Eye.

The size of the pupil diameter changes from small to big or vice versa based on the number of lights entering the eye. Factors that make the size of the pupil vary are age, disease, health condition or trauma.

The iris is another key component of the eye that plays a crucial part in human vision and responsible for controlling the diameter and size of the pupil. The iris structure section explains in brief about the iris architecture, unique micro-characteristics and the criteria that determine the iris as a suitable human template to be used in the biometric system.

2.2 IRIS STRUCTURE

The iris consists of strong muscles that contract or expand to control the amount of light entering a person's eye. The muscles control the permitted lights from reaching the sensory tissue of the retina and prevent a person from eye strain due to too much glare from bright light or sunlight.

Inside the iris, there is another layer of two thin sheets of muscles, called the pupillary and ciliary zones. On top of the muscle zones, lie layers of blood vessels that have their own functions and capabilities.

Surprisingly, the pupillary zone contains two more thin sheets of muscles, which are pupillary frill and pupillary ruff. The magical pupillary frill also known as collarette helps to determine the termination of the pigment layer. Collarette is a narrow rim of loosened keratin overhanging the periphery of a circumscribed skin lesion and located in between the pupillary and ciliary zones (Alora, 2015). Meanwhile, the pupillary ruff provides a margin of the posterior pigment near the pupillary margin. The pupillary ruff controls the pupil dilations, which make the iris smaller and pupil size larger under dim light conditions. Generally, every human's pupil size changes from 2 millimetres to 8 millimetres (Bianco, 2015 and Norma Ramirez, 2018) according to the amount of light entering the eyes. However, the pupillary zone shows no variation in iris features especially in short durations of time, before the next iris image capture (Hao Chen et al., 2017).

On the other hand, the ciliary zone performs pupil shrinking yet the iris is larger, under a bright light condition (Hande Husniye Telek et al., 2018). The iris sizes vary between 4 millimetres to 10 millimetres due to the amount of light that enters the eyes. The interior of the ciliary zone consists of several layers of blood vessels characterized by crypts, furrows (Forrester et al., 2008) and collarette, which determine the authenticity of a person. The unique information of features inside the iris also shows the different characteristics from person to person.

The crypt contains several smaller diamond-shaped crypts in various sizes (Baker et al., 2019) and they are found in black, pinprick holes that puncture to the deepest level, which are easily detected from a distance (Elizabeth Sidhartha, 2014). The crypt is a combination of ciliary zone and layers of blood vessels presented in complex but nicely arranged tangled crystals in clear view. Figure 2 illustrates the crypt.

Furrow is another blob of iris features that are represented as concentric muscles, looking like rings around the outer edge of the iris. The muscle controls the contraction and dilation of the pupil and has a wrinkled look. Moreover, furrows start to shrink or expand at the pupil

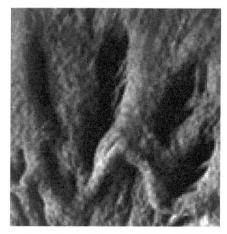

Figure 2: Crypt (Ann-Marie Baker, 2019).

edge towards the outer iris edge. Furrows are typically disjointed and flabbergasted across the iris (Melissa Edwards et al., 2016). Figure 3 shows the furrow shape.

Furrows tend to fold in the same location according to different light conditions (Sturm and Larsson, 2009). Moreover, the contraction and dilation of the furrow are based on the thickness and melanocyte density of the iris. In fact, the furrows' ripple shapes and movement of contractions and dilations are dependent on genes from previous

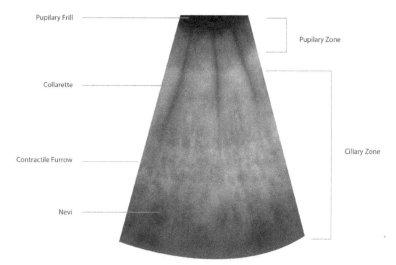

Figure 3: Furrow (Sturm and Larsson, 2009).

ancestors. For instance, furrows of Asians have more thickness and higher melanocyte density and shape compared to Europeans. The iridial stromal melanocytes have revealed that differences in perceived eye colour are the result of variable amounts and qualities of the melanosome particles in which the melanin pigment is packaged within these cells.

Another blob of iris feature is freckled and only some individuals may have it (Andrian A. Lahola-Chomiak and Michael A. Walter, 2018). The increase of pigmentation occurs when an individual has a disease such as a gastric ulcer in the stomach and medical cases (Ann-Marie Baker et al., 2019) or exposure to sunlight for a long time. It is also called iris nevus or iris ephelis.

A rare case of pigment blotches shows the individual's diseased condition of the kidney or cancer. Iridology is another branch of study, which throws light on human diseases based on the health of the eye.

Despite the authentic blob or micro characteristics appearing in the iris, its colour presents the genetics transmission, which is inherit from a person. Coloured irises are based on pigmentation (Wielgus and Sarna, 2005) and frequency-dependence of the scattering of light in the stroma of the iris. The pigmentation relies on the melanin in the epithelium pigment, the melanin content in the stroma and the cellular density of the stroma (Wang et al., 2006).

The epithelium pigment is located at the back of the iris, meanwhile, the melanin content is located at its front. The thicker the melanin the darker the colour of the iris would be. The colour of the iris comes is a result of the scattering of light entering the stroma and the presence of other pigments such as purines, pteridines and carotenoids inside it. There are many iris colours such as blue, green, grey, hazel, brown and dark brown, which inherit from the same race or diversity due to multi-racial marriages that make the colour of the iris another important feature. Blue eye colour presents low melanin content and thinner melanocyte density inside the irises, which causes it to reflect light instead of absorbing it into the eye, which is called Tyndall effect.

Moreover, the layers of tiny blood vessels and thin sheets of muscles inside the iris create beautiful colour and patterns to distinguish a person from another person. Amazingly, the pattern of the iris is unique and the accuracy value is not the same from one person to another person. Just imagine how many people are living in this world but each person has a different iris pattern for the left and right eye. This is incredible.

From all the micro-characteristics and colour of the iris, crypts and furrows are the most authentic blobs of iris features since they are influenced by human growth or aging (Poonguzhali and Ezhilarasa,

2015) and genetic traits that are useful for iris recognition in the biometric system.

2.3 THE USE OF IRIS FOR BIOMETRIC SYSTEM

The story of an Afghani girl who fascinates a cameraman's attention with her beautiful eyes who captured her photo at the refugee camp has inspired the development of iris recognition for biometric systems. After 10 years, the cameraman recognized the lady whose photo he took just from the colour and texture of her eyes. Since then, medical doctors, pioneered the work of (Flom and Safir, 1987), and later followed by Professor Dr. John Daugman who started working on iris recognition systems.

The motivation that drives researchers to work on the iris is its highly individualizing authentic DNA in an individual's left and right eyes and in identical twins that is useful for iris recognition in biometric systems (Alora Sansola, 2015). The biological and behavioral characteristics of an individual from repeatable features can be extracted for the biometric iris recognition systems (Jagadeesh and Patil, 2017) and (Khotimah and Juniati, 2018).

Also, studies (Norma Ramirez et al., 2018), (Mancino et al., 2018) indicate that the blob inside the iris is highly distinctive (Rawate et al., 2017), (Yung-Hui Li, 2017), stable (Daugman, 2014), and unique (Omran and Al-Hilali, 2018), (Bramhananda Reddy et al., 2018) throughout a person's lifetime (Daugman and Cathryn Downing, 2015), (Poonguzhali and Ezhilarasan, 2015) and (Zhao, 2018) although each iris structure is from the eyes of the same person.

On the other hand, Alora stated that the iris recognition system is on average 80% accurate (Alora, 2015). The iris colour does not influence recognition performance and accuracy much since 57% accuracy in blue or grey irises and 82% in brown coloured ones is observed. Thus, for iris recognition, it is better to store the iris image in a grayscale or monochrome image to avoid bias and to achieve standard performance accuracy between various datasets.

Even though the iris image is monochromatic, it still exhibits a high noise rate. The iris image with a high noise rate affects the segmentation process (Prajoy et al., 2018) that influences the accuracy of the result. The non-important information that comes from surrounding parts of the eye such as eyelids, eyelashes, retina and flashlight from the camera produce an occlusion, which hides the crucial information about the iris and creates a high noise rate problem in the iris template for the recognition process.

2.4 SUMMARY

Every human has a pair of beautiful and incredible eyes. The eye is an internal organ of the human body that is viewed from the outside. The human eye consists of complex components such as lens, retina, cornea, pupil and iris, which each has its functions. However, the iris is the crucial component in the eye for human vision since it controls the amount of light entering the eye. The iris performs as an elastic sheet to control the tightening and expansion movements that make the pupil look smaller and bigger. The reason is to prevent a glaring condition and giving a good human vision. Surprisingly, the iris is layered with tiny blood vessels, thin muscles and melanin that produce stunning colour and unique patterns for an individual. The pattern of the iris feature is authentic and different from one person to another. Iris from the left side and right side of the eye contains different patterns even though from the same person. Therefore, the authentic iris motivates researchers to use it as a bio-key for the iris recognition in access control systems. Chapter 3 discusses more on the iris problems in the first generation of iris recognition.

The First Phase of Iris Recognition

Chapter 3 describes the early development of iris recognition. The first phase of iris recognition systems explains the fundamental phases and processes involved in the creation of IrisCodes. The basic component of the iris recognition system involves image acquisition, segmentation, normalization, extraction and comparison. The first phase sees new areas of research and dealing with problems in biometric applications and concentrates on circular segmentation techniques like Integral Daugman Operator (IDO), Hough Transform (HT), Principal Component Analysis (PCA) and wavelets (DCT, DWT, FFT). This is done to store the iris template in the form of binary codes from the process of compression and encoding technique for matching, the real-time iris template with the stored iris template for comparison to find a successful match. The matching technique used for the first generation of iris recognition is the Hamming Distance in following the standard of implementation for biometrics worldwide.

3.1 OVERVIEW

In 1936, the iris recognition concept was initially proposed by an ophthalmologist, Dr. Frank Earl Burch. The idea was patented by two other ophthalmologists, Dr. Leonard Flom and Aran Safir in 1987 (Leonard Flom and Aran Safir, 1987). Later, in 1992, Dr. Flom collaborated with Dr. John Daugman, a physicist and computer expert, to develop an automated iris recognition system (Tobji et al., 2018). Iris recognition algorithms were proposed by Daugman (2016) and have been successfully used for commercial applications.

Daugman's approach has been used as a model of reference for iris recognition systems in biometrics. The rationale for using it is that it has been tested in the real environment, and involves gigantic databases and procedures worldwide (Daugman, 2016). Biometric recognition means an automated recognition of individuals that implies a machine-based system either with a full process or assisted by a human being during the matching phase, to determine whether the match is genuine or fake. The iris is selected for biometric recognition according to its accuracy, reliability, and permanence (Christina-Angeliki Toli and Bart Prencel, 2018).

In Daugman's approach, there are four main phases in the existing iris recognition system. Firstly, in the image acquisition phase, the eye image is captured (480 × 640) using a camera or a near-infrared sensor. The iris region is located in the annular form of the eye image to differentiate between the pupil and iris regions, which are called "unwrapped".

Secondly, in the segmentation phase, the coordinates of the raw image (x,y) inside the unwrapped are marked with degree measure of angle, radius and direction of circular movement. The marked unwrapped coordinates are converted into normalized polar coordinates (r, θ), where r is the radius ranging from 0 to 1; and θ ranges from 0 to 2π, which is named as the 'rubber sheet model' in a rectangular shape (20 × 240). A texture filter is applied to the normalized iris image.

Thirdly, important features in the normalized iris are obtained and encoded in the feature extraction phase. The complex filter responses are quantized to create an IrisCode in a binary form. Each complex number is represented as two bits in the IrisCode. The first bit is a "1" if the real part of the number is positive, and "0" otherwise; similarly, the second bit is a "1" if the imaginary part of the number is positive, and "0" otherwise. As a result, this process creates an IrisCode as the biometric template to be stored in the database.

Fourthly, the real-time IrisCode is compared in the comparison phase with the stored IrisCode to identify if the user is accepted or rejected by the system and a decision is based on the fractional Hamming Distance (the fraction of bits that disagree).

The iris recognition model as shown in Figure 4 provides a framework for any inventor, biometrics user, community and developer to standardize the proposed design or model or algorithm for worldwide use. Furthermore, the iris recognition system consists of two main phases; enrolment and comparison.

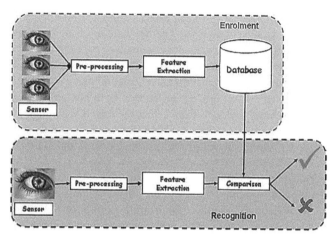

Figure 4: Iris Biometric System Phase (Junhyoung Oh et al., 2019).

3.2 ENROLMENT PROCESS

The enrolment is a process to create biometric captured data and transforming it into a biometric template following the biometric enrolment policy, which consists of iris image acquisition, pre-processing and extraction processes. Then, the biometric template is stored in the database for further matching processes.

3.2.1 Image Acquisition and Iris Database

The iris image acquisition phase involves hardware and software specifications that measure the blurriness and off-angle image captured from the camera or iris sensor (near infrared or thermal). The environment (indoor or outdoor) contributes to either a good or bad quality (noisy) such iris images. Unsuitable camera settings at certain distances in the acquisition stage may also add to higher error rates. There are four types of cameras for iris acquisition, such as access control, handheld, dual-eye visor, and stand-off portal and each has its advantages and disadvantages. The camera's distance may be short or long or remote, and the iris may be static or moving. Additionally, the amount of light that enters the eye contributes to giving different diameter values of the pupil and the iris. Subsequently, the images acquired by the camera or sensor, are either high or low quality and stored in the iris database.

Iris self-captured public databases and iris database provider shares of eye images are available for other researchers to perform experiments and validation. The offered databases need to be downloaded from the

CASIA (Chinese Academy of Sciences' Institute of Automation) from China, UBIRIS (Noisy Visible Wavelength Iris Image Databases) produced by SOCIA Lab—Soft Computing and Image Analysis Group, Department of Computer Science, the University of Beira Interior, Portugal, Iris Databases, Multimedia University Malaysia (MMU Iris database), IIT Delhi Iris Database and Iris Registry.

The images are stored in .jpg, .bmp or .png format. For each person, both the left and the right eyes were enrolled separately. Users of the public dataset need to register and fill up the agreement forms before the eye images are downloaded.

Iris images of CASIA-Iris-Interval were captured with the iris camera designed with a circular NIR LED array, with suitable luminous flux for iris imaging and well-suited for detecting the detailed iris image texture features.

For one eye, seven to ten images were captured during the two different sessions. It should be noted that most of the images in CASIA databases have been captured from Asian people, in which the upper eyelid position is generally low. The eyelids and eyelashes might cover some portion of the iris pattern, which degrades the recognition rate. Thus, it is assumed that the iris images have been segmented and normalized without enhancing the contrast in the experiments.

A majority of the open databases incorporate a few noise types, almost exclusively related to eyelid and eyelash obstructions. However, the UBIRIS database (Proenca and Alexandre, 2005) tries to simulate non-cooperative imaging conditions. It captures images with heterogeneous characteristics of focus, motion blur, contrast, brightness, as well as iris occlusions by eyelids or eyelashes, specular and lighting reflections. Due to these characteristics, the UBIRIS version 1 database was chosen to be used in this work. The experimental tests, aimed to approach a more realistic situation, which made the iris pre-processing further challenging such that the systems required the subjects to stand close (less than two meters) to the imaging camera and look for about three seconds until the data was captured. This cooperative behaviour is required to capture images with enough clarity for the recognition task. On the other hand, it simultaneously restricts the range of domains where iris recognition can be applied, especially those where the subjects' cooperation is not expected (e.g., criminal/terrorist seeks, and missing children).

The main focus of the UBIRIS.v1 database is to minimize the requirement of user cooperation, to provide automatic recognition of individuals, using images of their iris captured at-a-distance; and minimizing the required degree of cooperation from the users, probably even in a covert mode.

The iris images collected at this stage simulated the ones captured by a vision system with or without minimal active participation from the subjects, adding several noise problems. Due to the simulated properties provided by CASIA.v3 (for high quality images) and UBIRIS.v1 (noisy iris images) both databases were able to replicate the real environment in different conditions. The experiential environment acts as the testbed for further testing, evaluation and validation for the proposed approach in extraction and matching phases.

3.2.2 Circular Segmentation and Normalization

In iris segmentation, the pupil and iris boundaries are localized and the process of contouring the iris starts from the inner to the outer part of the iris. Daugman's Integro-Differential Operator (IDO) and Hough Transform (HT) are common techniques to segment the iris.

The first approach, IDO, is based on the illumination difference between the inside and the outside boundaries of pixels in the iris edge circle. In other words, the difference in the values of the pixels' grey level gives a higher value than any other pixel in images which turns colours into white. The equation for locating the inner and outer boundaries of an iris. The operator is applied iteratively with the amount of smoothing being progressively reduced to attain precise localization.

$$max(r, x_0, y_0) \mid G\sigma(r) * \frac{\delta}{\delta r} \oint_{r, x0, y0} \frac{I(x, y)}{2\pi r} \, ds \mid$$

where,

(x, y) = image domain for the maximum in the blurred partial derivative

$I(x,y)$ = normalized contour integral iris

$2\pi r$ = Perimeter of the circle

r = radius

x_0, y_0 = centre coordinates image domain of blurred partial derivative

ds = a small contour element along a circular arc

$G \delta(r)$ = Gaussian smoothing function

s = contour of the circle of radius r with the centre at (x_0, y_0)

$\frac{\delta}{\delta r}$= change in pixel values when there is a variation of the radius and the x and y coordinates.

The Hough Transform (HT) aims to recognize the circles presented in an image. This approach is used to obtain the parameters that define the circle that represents the pupil border and the circle that represents the external iris border. The process starts by converting the grey-scaled eye image into a binary edge map. Then, the construction of the edge map is accomplished by the Canny edge detection method with the incorporation of gradient information.

The HT procedure requires the generation of a vote accumulation matrix with the number of dimensions equal to the number of parameters necessary to define the geometric form. For a circle, the accumulator has 3 dimensions, namely x, y and r. Each edge pixel with coordinates (x, y) in the image space is mapped for the parameter space, determining two of the parameters (for example, x_c and y_c) and finding the third one (for example, r), which resolves the circumference.

$$(x - x_c)^2 + (y - y_c)^2 = r^2$$

As a result, the point with coordinates (xc, yc, r) is obtained in the parameter space, which represents a possible circle in the image. At each set of parameters obtained (xc, yc, r), the value of accumulator at the position of $A(xc, yc, r)$ is incremented. When all the pixels have been processed, the highest value of the accumulator A indicates the parameters of probable circles in the image. Therefore, the Hough Transform searches the optimum pixels in the image of the iris template.

$$H(xc, yc, r) = \Sigma_{i=1}^{n} h(xi, yi, xc.yc, r)$$

Segmentation is a process of creating contour sections from the starting to the endpoint of the iris shape with 360° rotation. The pupil, eyelashes, and eyelids are removed from the space. On the other hand, Bachoo uses principal component analysis (PCA) to remove the noise and redundancy (Bachoo et al., 2004). Then the Hough Transform technique is applied to find the circular iris. Other algorithms can be used for iris segmentation for instance, Lim combines Haar wavelet and a neural network to achieve iris recognition (Lim et al., 2001). There are two types of segmentation techniques, in which the entire iris texture is segmented and partial segmentation is performed. The entire iris texture has been segmented using the circular format of the iris texture regardless of the presence of noise (eyelids, eyelashes, and occlusions) since it represents the person's vital information. On the other hand, the partial iris texture has been segmented by applying the mask and white noise to reduce the noise. Noise reduction in segmentation leads to a higher performance accuracy.

Two established algorithms have been widely used in commercial iris biometric applications, which are the Integro-Differential Operator and Hough Transform. The experiments done by (Zainal Abidin et al., 2012) showed that the Hough Transform performed better compared to Integro-Differential Operator in terms of noise tolerance in the noisy iris. However, the existing techniques are unable to cater to the segmented iris when it is off-angle and occluded.

Concerning image processing, the noise in the iris is reduced in many ways, which are deblurring the use of white noise in circular or non-circular format and image enhancement.

The deblurring technique is the blur motion technique applied to the iris image that has been blurred due to camera settings and the process is reversed to achieve a better quality iris image (De Almeida, 2017). Another approach to reducing the amount of noise in the iris image is applying white noise to the iris image and removing the noise from the iris texture images (Ali et al., 2016) and (Min Beom Lee et al., 2017). The iris image enhancement (Hassan et al., 2017) is applied for better comparison.

The next step after the iris segmentation in the pre-processing phase is the normalization. The normalization is the phase-based extraction process, which extracts the important binary feature vectors from the segmented iris and encoded them to be the iris code. This process is crucial since the iris code is stored in the database and used for future matching processes. Moreover, the extraction process involves encoding and feature selection sub-processes.

Subsequently, upon the completion of segmentation, the normalization process is executed that aims to transform the annular region of the iris to a rectangular shape, which is uniformly sampled in the radial direction from the polar coordinate representation to a pixel convolution space format. This process is important for solving the problem of dimensional inconsistencies that are generally provoked by the variation of the distance between the individual and the image capturing device and also by the variation of the size of the pupil due to the varying levels of the luminosity of the environment. The most utilized normalization method is called the "rubber sheet model", which measures the range of pixel intensity and binary values using a suitable technique to identify the uniqueness in each iris. Figure 5 illustrates the iris normalization process.

In addition, iris normalization under the Hough Transform method uses the phase-based feature extraction method with a one-dimensional (1D) Gabor wavelet for iris template generation, which is based on polar coordinates and a logarithmic frequency scale. The phase-based feature extraction technique captures the round shaped image of the iris and arranges it in a rectangular table in a zig-zag movement from left

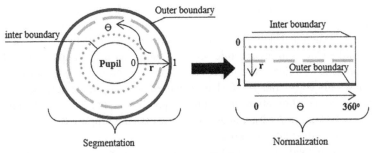

Figure 5: Iris Normalization.

to right. The mathematical form of 1D log polar Gabor filter (Glpr) is described as,

$$Glpr = exp\ (-2\pi^2\sigma^2\ (ln(r-r_0/f))^2\tau^2\ /\ (2ln(f_0\ sin\ (\theta-\theta_0))^2$$

where,

$$\sigma = \frac{1}{\pi ln(r0)\ sin(\pi/\theta0)}\ \frac{\sqrt{ln\ 2}}{2}$$

$$\tau = \frac{2\pi ln(r0)\ sin(\pi/\theta0)}{ln\ 2}\ \frac{\sqrt{ln\ 2}}{2}$$

where,

(r,σ) = polar coordinates

(r_0, θ_0) = initial values,

f = centre frequency of the filter

f_0 is the parameter that controls the bandwidth of the filter.

Several techniques available for the extraction process is discussed further in section 3.2.3.

3.2.3 Extraction

Four major groups of iris extraction have been applied for iris recognition, which are phase-based approaches (Solanke et al., 2017), zero crossing approaches (de Martin-Roche, 1998), (Sanchez-Avila, 2002), texture analysis based approaches (Neda Ahmadi et al., 2015) and intensity variation analysis-based approaches (Alice Nithya et al., 2017).

The first method in the extraction process is the phase-based approach, which is the binary representation of iris code. The iris code shows feature vectors corresponding to individual iris images. At the same time, the feature vectors perform iris matching based on some distance metrics, such as Hamming Distance. Furthermore, the Log-Gabor filter uses the Gaussian logarithmic scale technique used in the phase-based approach. Moreover, the improvement to the phase approach such as phase only correlation (POC) has been used due to its better performance accuracy. The limitation in the phase approach is that it cannot handle iris aging and noisy iris images, which causes the flipping bits problem to occur in the matching process.

The second method is the zero crossings approach applied in one dimensional wavelets for encoding the input images of iris features. The mother wavelet is defined as the second derivative of a smoothing

function $\theta(x)$ $\psi(x) = \dfrac{d^2\theta(x)}{dx^2}$

The zero crossings of dyadic filter scales are then used to encode features (Masek, 2003). The wavelet transforms of a signal f(x) at scale s and position x are given by

$$W_s f(x) = f * \left(s^2 \frac{d^2\theta(x)}{dx^2} \right)(x)$$

$$= s^2 \frac{d^2}{dx^2}(f * \theta_s)(x)$$

where

$\theta_s = (1/s)(x/s)$

$W_s f(x)$ is proportional to the second derivative of f(x) smoothed by $\theta_s(x)$, and the zero crossings of the transform correspond to points of inflection in $f*\theta_s(x)$. It represents iris features at different resolution levels based on the wavelet transform zero-crossing. The algorithm is used in translation, rotation and invariant scales. The wavelet function is the first derivative of the cubic spline. The centre and diameter of the iris are calculated from the edge-detected image. The virtual circles are constructed from the centre and stored as circular buffers. The information extracted from any of the virtual circles is normalized to have the same number of data points and a zero-crossing representation is generated. The representation is periodic and independent from the starting point on the virtual circles of the iris. These are stored in the database as iris signatures. The dissimilarity between the irises of the same eye images were smaller compared to the eye images of different eyes. The advantage of this function is that the amount of computation is reduced since the number of zero crossings is less than the number of data points.

However, the drawback is that it requires a comparison of representations to have the same number of zero crossings at each resolution level (Arrawatia et al., 2017). Meanwhile, the same process uses zero crossings of dyadic scales filters which is the motivation for this technique so that it corresponds to significant features within the iris region. A distance is directly related to the zero-crossing representation of a 1D signal that is computed using only the zero crossing points. The overall dissimilarity value of the unknown object and the candidate model over the resolution interval is the average of the dissimilarity functions calculated at each resolution level in this interval. The Dyadic Wavelet Transform is the improvement of the zero-crossing approach.

The third method is the texture analysis-based approach and (Hezil et al., 2015). High quality iris images were captured using a silicon intensified target camera coupled with a standard frame grabber and a resolution of 512×480 pixels. The limbus and pupil are modelled with circular contours which are extended to the upper and lower eyelids with parabolic arcs. The particular contour parameter values x, y and radius r are obtained by the voting of the edge points using Hough transformation. The largest number of edge points represents the contour of the iris. The Laplacian of Gaussian (LoG) is applied to the image at multiple scales and a Laplacian pyramid is constructed. The LoG filter is given as

$$-\frac{1}{\pi\sigma^2}\left(1-\frac{\rho^2}{2\sigma^2}\right)e^{\rho^2/2\sigma^2}$$

where σ is the standard deviation of the Gaussian and ρ is the radial distance of a point from the filter's centre.

The fourth extraction method is an intensity variation analysis-based approach. The iris intensity value is characterized by local intensity variations. The sharp variation points of iris patterns are recorded as features. In the iris localization phase, the centre coordinates of the pupil are estimated by image projections in the horizontal and vertical directions. The exact parameters of the pupil and iris circles are calculated using the Canny edge detection operator and Hough transform. The iris in Cartesian coordinate system is projected into a doubly dimensionless pseudo polar coordinate system. The local spatial patterns in an iris consist of frequency and orientation information. Gabor filters are constructed to acquire a frequency band in the spatial domain. Gabor functions are Gaussians modulated by circularly symmetric sinusoidal functions. The feature extraction begins by generating 1D intensity signals considering the information density in the angular direction.

The 1D signal is represented using a dyadic wavelet transform to obtain the feature vector. It decomposes the signal into detailed components at different scales. The feature values are the mean and the average absolute deviation of the magnitude of each 8×8 blocks in the filtered image with the total number of blocks being 768. For dimensionality reduction, Fisher Linear Discriminant is used and for classification, the nearest centre classifier is used. The similarity between the pair of feature vectors is calculated using the XOR operation. The circular shift-based matching is performed from which the minimum matching score is obtained after several circular shifts.

Alternatively, the orthogonal moment-based method is proposed (Kaur et al., 2018) and the Gauss-Hermite moments of 1D signals are used as distinguishing features. These moments are effective to characterize the local details of the signal. Ten intensity signals were generated and four different order (1–4) moments were used. The feature vector was constructed by concatenating these features. The nearest centre classifier based on cosine similarity measures was adopted for classification in a low dimensional feature space.

The GMM method was further improved (Othman, 2016), in which the local feature-based classifier was combined with an iris blob matcher. The blob matching aimed at finding similar spatial correspondences between the blocks in the input image and those in the stored model. The similarity is based on the number of matched block pairs. The block attributes are recorded as centroid coordinates, area and second order central moments.

The iris segmentation uses Daugman's method and the segmented image is normalized to 64×300 pixel dimensions. The feature extraction is performed using cumulative sums on groups of basic cells where each cell has a matrix size 3×10. The cell regions are grouped horizontally and vertically performing cumulative sums calculated over each group. The iris texture is generated based on the sum in both horizontal and vertical directions. For the summation values that lie between these two values, if the sum is on an upward slope and the cell's IrisCode is set to 1. When the sum is on the downward slope, the cell's IrisCode is set to 2 otherwise it is set to zero. Matching is performed using HD. The Gauss-Laguerre filter is used to generate a binary matrix similar to the IrisCode in the Daugman method (Arrawatia, 2017).

Once the normalized iris texture has been produced, the IrisCodes are stored in the database, either in a binary and or non-binary representation. The binary representation of IrisCode consists of binary bits and real and imaginary values are implemented in the encoding process. The binary bits of ones and zeros are in the 1024 kilobyte data representation. The

1k or 2k binary representatives use Hamming Distance. The encoding process transforms the iris texture into the IrisCode in a binary format.

Meanwhile, the non-binary representation of IrisCode is based on the image and intensity-based comparison. The IrisCode is stored in real and imaginary part values as illustrated in Figure 6. However, this approach consumes resources and computational processing time.

For the intensity and image-based approach, the IrisCodes are stored in image representations, either in RGB (red, green, blue) or grayscale format. The IrisCode is stored using histogram equalization in visualizing the pixel values inside the iris texture image of the Energy Histogram in the DCT sub-band (Drozdowski et al., 2018). On the other hand, the IrisCode database is indexed using energy histogram values in the DCT sub-band (Drozdowski et al., 2018). However, energy histogram values do not provide the information for unique iris features.

The IrisCode is generated after the encoding phase and the extracted iris is transformed into a stream of binary representations (binary format), which the computer easily understands. For the non-binary format of IrisCode, the image is catalogued and checked based on the tag number. Later, the IrisCode is stored in the database for the next verification or identification in the comparison phase.

Another method for storing information of non-binary presentation of IrisCode uses a compression technique (Devi et al., 2016). The purpose of compression is to provide smaller storage space, lightweight and a more secured image that provides minimal impact on the performance. Moreover, it saves the memory and energy of the computer. The compression technique available is JPEG 2000.

The Reverse Biorthogonal Wavelet Decomposition in the Compression Method (Paul et al., 2015) gives results showing that the percentage of coefficients before the compression of energy was 99.65%, and the number of zeros was 97.99%. However, the percentage of energy was increased to 99.97%, while the number of zeros remained unchanged after the compression, and the resulting impact produced different ratios with minimal loss. This finding indicates that the compression technique

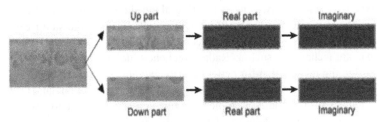

Figure 6: Real and Imaginary Parts of IrisCode (Biswas et al., 2017).

is an alternative way of converting the iris texture image into smaller sized IrisCode without losing too much information about the iris. The IrisCode created could be easily stored into a database on the cloud or any local server or transmitted using data communication channels (such as wired or wireless) or temporarily saved on the carrier (such as a smart card). The stored IrisCode is crucial since it is further used for the comparison process in finding a successful match with the real-time IrisCode.

Another method for keeping the non-binary IrisCode presentation information of the iris texture is transformed into pixel values using the Markov model. The pixel value of the iris texture image was arranged in a linear array and the Signed Pixel Level Difference Histogram (SPLDH) stored the raw pixel intensities into the database. Nonetheless, a proper index is needed since a database needs to store the pixel values of IrisCode together with the iris texture image's number. The benefit of using this approach is it speeds up the comparison but increases the computational processes.

A lot of techniques are available for saving the IrisCode either in the form of binary or pixel-values, nevertheless, the iris template demands a secure carrier and safe location for storing the crucial biometric data. It is foremost to safeguard the stored iris template due to data security and user privacy considerations. Thus, a suitable place to store the iris template is needed for the preparation of the next comparison process. More explanations about iris template storage are discussed in Section 3.3.

3.3 IRIS TEMPLATE STORAGE

The generated IrisCode also known as the iris template is stored in physical media in the form of a passport, a driving license, electronic keys and smart cards for example, which makes the individual verification process easier and faster (Boriev et al., 2016). However, physical media can be lost, duplicated, misplaced and stolen. Physical media storage is expensive and the users need to bring along the biometric smart card for biometric readers to verify their identities. Besides, the smart card feature is added with Near Fields Communication (NFC) and other relevant technology such as Radio Frequency Identification (RFID) for storing the information for better security and good performance. Users have their data privacy and are in charge of their identification data. One drawback of the biometric implementation is higher cost due to devices required to read the biometric data and information on the smart cards.

An alternative way of storing the iris template is by directly scanning the biometric data such as fingerprints on the sensing device, as in the form of a password. The sensing device provides a quick response in between the scanning process and the authentication process. However, it is not effective in situations where the user needs to authenticate at multiple locations. For example, when a biometric system is implemented for a computer lab, the frequency of readings at the sensors is high since the security officer cannot assume that each user is going to be working with the same machine and the same sensing device. Issues of hardware cost, the computation speed and a smaller design for the sensing device are considered for preventing easy theft of the device.

Another way of storing the iris template is in a central repository on a server in order to overcome the problem of users authenticating from multiple locations. However, there is a potential for a "sniffing" attack of the biometric data of the network and replaying the authentication session, unless encryption is used. Even when encryption is used, the question is where would the encryption keys be stored and who would have access to them. Thus the idea of information such as fingerprint data being stored centrally is not welcomed by privacy-conscious users. Nonetheless, if the iris template is stored in the cloud, privacy may not be an issue due to multiple access, faster data transmission and more security.

The individual workstations seem to be a reasonable middle ground between storage in central databases and sensing devices. On the other hand, a computer tower is physically more difficult to steal than a small sensing device. To store data distributively does create fewer privacy concerns and prevents a focal point of attack for malicious hackers. With workstation storage, however, the user cannot authenticate from multiple locations. Another issue is lack of security since the biometric data could be found on the hard drive and once it is stolen by a burglar then the biometric data is prone to manipulation for illegal use.

If you are a user of a smartphone, you might use your fingerprint to unlock your phone. The biometric data is stored in your phone and used for authentication especially when using mobile banking. The purpose is to reduce the risk of data leakage during the data transmission and provides a data security environment. On the other hand, internet-of-things (IoT) is considered for modern smartphones, tablets and door access cameras, which are designed to send or receive alerts and the biometric data is saved in the cloud for verification. Nonetheless, smart phones and IoT lack standards of data privacy and less effort are required to acquire data with inside or outside cyber-attacks.

Closed-circuit televisions (CCTVs) and surveillance cameras monitor day to day activities in a large area or a city. The huge data streaming in terabytes stores the human gait or facial expressions in the form of video frames which are located in the databases managed by Enterprise Security Management (ESM). However, a gigantic installation and integration between various monitoring tools need to be implemented phase by phase since the cost is enormous. The performance of video streaming and image quality is improved through a lot of research done by researchers.

The next section explains the comparison process, which finds the similarities of feature vectors in the iris database (stored as the iris template) and the newly captured iris texture (real-time iris template) to determine the genuine.

3.4 COMPARISON PROCESS

The comparison phase involves a re-enrolment process in obtaining the real-time iris template and comparing it with the stored iris texture template in the database. There are two modes of comparison which are identification and verification which involve the alignment and matching processes. Techniques used in matching consist of Hamming Distance (HD), normalized correlation, weighted Euclidean Distance, and Classifier (SVM, RVM and Adaboost).

The matching is based on a normalized correlation between the acquired and database images. Classification is performed using Fisher's linear discriminant function. The method for iris identification (Biu et al., 2018) uses a hybrid method for iris segmentation, Hough Transform for outer iris boundary and Integro-Differential operator for inner iris boundary. The iris code is produced using wavelet packets. The whole image is analyzed at different resolutions. 832 wavelets with 4 scales are used to generate 1664 bits code. The iris database consisted of 700 images acquired with visible light. An improvement of 2% FAR and 11.5% FRR was obtained compared to the Daugman method. It was observed that by considering colour information, an overall improvement of 2% to 10% was obtained according to the threshold value (Arrawatia et al., 2017).

A match would prove if the person is the same one, whose iris was enrolled earlier (Kapoor and Rawat, 2017). According to Daugman (John Daugman, 2015) at least 50% of the iris must be visible, or an HD of 0.3 with a minimum radius of 70 pixels should be captured in determining the iris pattern to classify authentication attempts into the classes of genuine or fake. The mode of comparison is explained in Section 3.4.1 for identification and Section 3.4.2 for verification.

3.4.1 Identification (Comparison for One-to-Many)

In the identification mode, the iris recognition system is trained by the same iris from several samples of a person. For each person, a biometric template is calculated in the training stage. A pattern that is going to be identified is matched against every known template, yielding either a score or a distance describing the similarity between the pattern (real-time) and the template (stored). The system assigns the pattern to the person with the most similar biometric template. To prevent impostor patterns from being correctly identified, the similarity has to exceed a certain level.

If this level is not reached, the pattern is rejected. In this method, no PIN or card is required. The reader performs an exhaustive search of the database in the central data which is stored to identify the user positively. However, the problem in the existing iris recognition failure-to-match problem appears when the recognition system rejects a genuine user.

3.4.2 Verification (Comparison for One-to-One)

"Two Factor Authentication" or "Strong Authentication" allows one to verify if the person presenting the card (or entering the correct PIN access code) is an authorized user, and not someone using a stolen card or compromised PIN. This is called iris authentication, and it involves biometric security in tightening the security from the intruder who tries to pose as a genuine person.

In the verification case, a person's identity is claimed a priori. The pattern that is verified is compared with the person's template. Similar to identification, whether the similarity between the pattern and the template is sufficient is checked to provide access to the secured system. To verify that a person is who he or she claims to be, a camera image is taken again and a new IrisCode is generated. Later, a comparison is made between the IrisCode that has just been created and a single IrisCode on a smart token or in the database (Kapoor and Rawat, 2017).

However, pattern matching can be enhanced to obtain a faster matching speed, stated by Yuan (Hudaib, 2016) that the matching is based on coefficients between the stored template and the real iris template. The value of the threshold is also important in determining the error rate for measuring the performance accuracy, wavelet, embedding zero tree and curvelet transform.

During matching, template alignment is performed within a single dimension, applying a circular shift of IrisCode. The main reason for shifting one of the two paired IrisCode is to obtain a perfect alignment to tolerate a certain amount of relative rotation between the two iris textures.

Consequently, the performance accuracy underwent degradation since the information of the iris texture (in binary bits) was not the same as the real-time user (noisy or unstable iris) (Hala N. Fathee et al., 2019). The iris information inside the iris code creates 'flipping bits' in the matching process, which means that bit '0' is changed to '1' and vice versa. The average fragility for each template is not correlated with the number of images for the template (Hollingsworth et al., 2007).

Therefore, the experts have diverted their attention to noisy and non-cooperative iris recognition, which brings challenges in the next generation of iris recognition. This high noise rate iris problem generates intriguing and open-ended questions to ponder over. The question is what shape of iris feature is unique in determining the genuine although with a high noise rate of distortion in the image.

3.5 CHALLENGES IN THE FIRST PHASE OF IRIS RECOGNITION

Challenges in iris recognition come from various factors such as cost, threats and attacks; hardware and software limitations; distorted iris; iris at a distance; handling poor quality data and feature selection with a bio-inspired algorithm as shown in Figure 7. Moreover, iris feature changes and occlusions are two major problems under highly distorted images.

However, distortion in iris features (Mingyang Wang et al., 2017) is influenced by human factors such as aging, growth, health conditions, emotional state, diet, and eye laser surgery. In reality, the distortion caused the change or variation in iris features (Mateusz Trokielewicz, 2015). They develop over time and usually build up slowly (Mateusz Trokielewicz et al., 2017). On the other hand, it has been discovered that the aging or a certain growth leads to the iris recognition failure to match over time (Duncan Graham-Rowe, 2019). Moreover, various iris features, such as freckles, pigment blotches, and colours, also change with time. The change in iris features are classified according to the texture (fine, fine/medium, medium/coarse, coarse) and colour (blue/grey, amber, light brown, brown, dark brown). The regulation of pupil size is not only for controlling light levels, but it is a response to optical, neurological, and emotional factors mediated by the autonomic nervous system (Hall

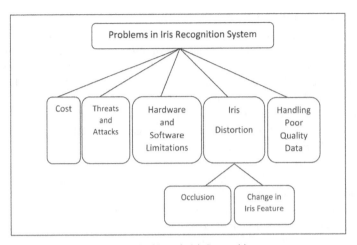

Figure 7: Problems in Iris Recognition.

Charlotte et al., 2018). On the other hand, the iris information may differ and the features are stretched in size during normal light. Besides, as the dim light source enters the eye, the pupil size gets bigger and covers some of the iris features. At the same time, the iris features are stretched to a larger size where it is not the same as under the condition of bright light. The situation of iris muscle contraction makes the comparison phase difficult to match between the stored binary representations with the real iris binary codes. As a result, the iris texture produces different information when the light is normal, bright and dim as in Figure 8.

The type of light entering the eye forces the iris movement to be either shrinking or expanding and directly affects the performance accuracy. Thus, the pattern of the iris template will give the same value for all bits during the matching process every time a comparison is conducted. The

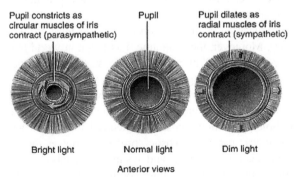

Figure 8: Pupillary zone contraction due to light source (Swihura, 2013).

reason for different matching values occurs due to the complex filter responses near the complex plane axes that produce the "fragile bits" situation in the IrisCode. A small rate of noise in the iris image changes the filter response from one quadrant to the adjacent quadrant that causes the particular bit in the IrisCode to flip, which is called "fragile". There is a probability of the fragile bit ending with "0" for some iris images and "1" for other iris images due to inconsistency in imaginary and real bits. Assume that the complex numbers associated with two bits of the IrisCode are close to the positive real axis.

Therefore, to enhance the performance accuracy, the fragile mask bits need to be identified. If the complex coefficient has a real part close to "0", then the mask corresponds to the real bit in the iris Code. However, if the complex coefficient has an imaginary part close to "0", then, the mask corresponds to the imaginary bit. The mask bits need to be 25% consistently on the complex numbers and closest to the axes. A good strategy is to focus on the separation between the genuine and fake distributions of Hamming Distance Scores to achieve better performance accuracy.

3.5.1 Cost of Biometrics System

Biometrics have been widely used in electronic devices at government workplaces, large enterprises and public sectors for human identification or verification. Biometric implementation produces an efficient process of authentication and an effective way of huge data handling (Indrayani, 2014). Even though biometrics technology is welcomed by the industry, however, the cost of the systems is high (Rui and Yan, 2019). According to Boriev, the cost of iris and face biometric system is among the highest in the market (Boriev et al., 2016).

For large enterprises, the overall expenditure of the organization does not get affected by the cost of the biometrics system. On the other hand, for small and medium-sized enterprises, the high cost of biometric systems produces an economic impact on long term sustainability in the industry. Moreover, the economic fluctuation in world trade creates uncertainty in financial planning for the small, micro and medium organizations in their struggle for business survival.

The deployment of biometrics system in small, micro and medium businesses demand a systematic selection and evaluation to determine the best choice. Additional costs are incurred for system applications such as biometric hardware sensors, processing power for maintaining database verification, research and testing, installation, infrastructure integration of user training, troubleshooting support, and productivity losses due to system calibration and system maintenance (Van Der Haar and Solms, 2014). Furthermore, the systematic selection of the authentication method is carried out based on the security requirements and the allocated funds (Boriev et al., 2016).

There is a lack of studies on finding solutions to reduce the sensor price, search for an alternative material for hardware development and less work on biometric awareness programs for making biometric systems affordable for use in small businesses. Small businesses have limited resources and inadequate mechanisms. Considering these factors researchers need to think of designing and developing new biometric systems with ease of maintenance, cost reduction and high accuracy. Since small companies cannot afford multiple trait-based biometric systems due to a strict budget.

3.5.2 Threats and Attacks in Biometrics

In biometric security, the biometric template encounters potential threats and attacks at security points and phases of the biometric system. Studies have shown that the man-in-the-middle is the attacker and phishing in web-based biometric authentication systems is a common attacking technique (Zeitz et al., 2008).

Ratha mentioned that the biometric system is exposed to attacks and threats by the intruder or impostor at several points and stages such as fake biometric and digital data, substitution attacks, masquerades and tampering (Ratha et al., 2003) (Ratha et al., 2005). Fake biometric data happens when an impostor gains access to a biometric system using fake data on the sensor. This kind of attack is commonly referred to as "spoofing". Meanwhile, fake digital data manipulates the real data by injecting the attack during data transmission between the sensor and the extraction process. In a substitute attack, the impostor replaces the registered user's identity with his or her own identity to access the biometric system. The masquerade attack is a technique to gain access to a biometric system by reconstructing the original biometric data that has been stolen from the database and synthesizing it to achieve similar matching scores. Tampering is an attack that gains access to the biometric system and overwrites the final decision that is either genuine or fake, achieved from the matching scores.

Another type of attack is the fake iris, which is a silicon or latex or A4 paper with the structure of the genuine user pre-printed on it to get access to the building (Eui Chul Lee et al., 2006). The intruder wears the silicon iris on the eye like a contact lens and looks at the sensor to access the gate. A fake iris attack is the simplest way to penetrate the access control system. Furthermore, another intruder put the pre-printed A4 paper with the iris template at the sensor and amazingly was granted access, indicating that this cheap hacking technique works.

3.5.3 Hardware and Software Limitations

The hardware architecture is not enough to support the software requirements that require higher speed and computation. The biometric system demands mobile applications, Internet-of-Things sensors (IoT) and cloud-based systems of access control for more reliable, accurate and fast response systems. With new technology coming into the systems, the execution and installation of the hardware request a lightweight device, smaller in size and easy to maintain if broken or stolen. Instead, the software application with an Artificial Intelligence (AI) algorithm consumes the computational process and memory of the hardware in producing a good user interface.

Moreover, the cost of authentication in a mobile device should be considered for reducing the hardware challenges. Most mobile devices (such as mobile phones and smart bracelets) need limited resources of electricity, computing capability, storage space, and battery life but almost every smartphone user has the gadget. Therefore, it becomes essential to study biometric authentication methods and algorithms that can be implemented in wearable devices or even low-end devices with low computational requirements (Rui and Yan, 2019).

The hardware and software limitations occur when dealing with huge data processing and transmission along the communication channels. A good biometric system must follow the standard of the system, which is unique, repeatable, accessible, universal and acceptable (Rao et al., 2014).

3.5.4 Iris Distortion

The first problem is a good quality iris image captured in the enrolment phase which is important since the iris template is used for the matching phase. The miss-match problem will arise during verification when the quality of iris image is low and high in noise rate (Lei et al. 2003). A low quality iris image such as a blurred image, off-angle and heavy iris occlusion, decreases the performance accuracy (Kalka et al., 2006). The image quality test is crucial in biometrics due to system performance (recognition and segmentation) and interoperability. In addition, the iris sensor camera and the photography technique indirectly make an impact on the quality of the iris images, which contribute to higher cost for the development of iris recognition. Solutions for a cost-effective iris sensor camera with a pre-setting configuration are highly needed for large commercial distribution use.

3.5.4.1 Iris Occlusion

The second problem is the instance of iris occlusion due to the light source which emits light from the environment (indoor/outdoor) into the ciliary zone causing the contraction of iris muscles. When the light is bright, the pupil size is smaller and many iris features can be seen and more iris information can be obtained, however, when the light is dim, the pupil size is larger and fewer features appear and lesser information is available.

3.5.4.2 Change in Iris Feature

The third problem is iris distortion, in which the alteration occurred in the iris template due to illness (Norma Ramirez et al., 2018) and eye surgery (Trokielewicz, 2018) (Roberto Pineda and Tulika Chauhan, 2016). The disease makes the pupil dilated at an odd orientation and off angular angle. Figure 9 demonstrates that the disease or illness occurred on the iris surface before and after the surgery was done. The result shows that the size of the pupil has changed according to the medical prescription. Hamming Distance used for the matching phase is the change in average HD from 0.098 to 0.2094 and it gives an average visual score growth rate of 11.13%. Eye surgery is done to improve the size of the pupil. After the eye surgery, the iris features are not of the same size anymore nor in the same position.

The fourth problem is iris aging (Bowyer and Ortiz, 2015). The amount of melanin in the irises is reduced due to the aging factor and changes the eye colour. For example, if the colour of the eye is brown but as he or she is aging, the eye colour changes to light brown or hazel. Aging in the iris generates crypts and furrows in various shapes and sizes.

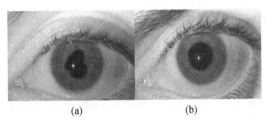

(a)   (b)

Figure 9: Images of the Iris with Disease or Illness in (a) Before Surgery and (a) After the Surgery (Aslam, 2009).

The fifth problem is occlusions happening when there are obstacles and it is not possible to find the important information of the iris template (Linsangan et al., 2019). It is due to eyelids, eyelashes, or eyebrows; the presence of specular highlights, strands of hair and contact lenses (Sheng-Hsun Hsieh, 2018) and (Yung-Hui Li et al., 2019), produce high error rates and give a low percentage value in performance accuracy.

Therefore, problems in iris distortion and occlusion in the first generation of iris recognition contribute to non-matching results during the matching process. In the matching phase, the iris template is compared with the other templates in the database. If the match is successful then the person is identified and for an unsuccessful match, the system rejects the unclear iris image and prevents the genuine person from accessing the commercial iris recognition systems (Zhang et al., 2018). The 'failure to match' does not produce a total failure of the iris recognition system but there is always a way to enhance the existing system. The failure to match condition is influenced by the error rate value. Each iris template has its own error rate value. The matching process is based on the error rate and the threshold value of the Hamming Distance comparison.

The other problems existing in identifying the genuine person in the iris recognition system are as under:

- High Noise Iris Template—In data acquisition of iris templates, high noise iris is generated from defective physical sensors and insufficient ambient conditions that produce them to be incorrectly matched or rejected (Abikoye et al., 2014).

- Intra-class variations—An iris template generated during the enrolment phase gives a different one in the verification phase. The resultant template from the matching process produces a dissimilar one in data representation format or an unsuccessful matching result (Young et al., 2019).

- Uniqueness—Every iris template is distinctive since it has an upper bound of discriminating characteristics during iris template generation (Ranjan et al., 2017).

- Non-universality—A portion of the generated iris template information does not present information about the person (Mohamed Basheer et al., 2018).

- Overriding biometric template in the database—security and privacy of the iris template in the database are hacked by intruders. Moreover, the biometric template is easily duplicated and shared in the database or other applications.

• Intellectual Property—Intellectual Property (IP) such as patents, copyrights and trademarks are another problem in iris recognition systems since most points of the security system in biometrics become vulnerable to cyber-attacks. The results show that the iris recognition system is insecure for those using it (Yang et al., 2019).

In addition, the first generation of automated iris recognition has been well accepted by the biometrics community, nevertheless, there is a lack of stability for long-term data collection (Li et al., 2018), system robustness, and good performance (Omran and Al-Hilali, 2018). The purpose of the second generation of iris recognition systems is to overcome the challenges in their first generation.

3.5.5 Handling Poor Quality Data

Dealing with the real-world deployment of biometric systems, biometric samples often suffer from various degradations, leading to acquired biometric data of different quality levels. When the capture is done under strict conditions (controlled mode), the samples are usually of good quality. However, an uncontrolled model, many factors such as user's behaviour, environmental conditions and sensor designs negatively affect the performance of the system (Nadia Othman et al., 2016).

Iris templates contain high noise rates and it is difficult to perform verification or identification. Blurred and unclear iris images produce a dissimilarity between the real-time and the stored iris template. Many techniques are used to reduce the noise such as the white noise application, noise removal and noise reduction.

The Quality of the iris template must be based on standards and metrics of evaluation. One needs to know the threshold value of acceptance that indicates to the iris recognition system the user is genuine or fake. From the metric measurements, the accuracy value is very crucial since it is used to decide either a successful or failed match. Meanwhile, the accuracy of the biometric system is determined by the threshold value. If the threshold is configured at a very low level, then, the system will reject many genuine users. Nonetheless, if the threshold is set at a high level, the system will freely allow impostors access.

The performance of biometric systems is dependent on the quality of the image. Ensuring a good quality iris image even in highly constrained imaging conditions with less visible light is a big challenge to the iris recognition system. A poor-quality iris image decreases the performance of the system and increases the false rejection rate (FRR).

Iris images with low quality lead to high dissimilarity (Mohsen Jenadeleh et al., 2020) and result in biometric system failure in the matching process.

Thus, methods to improve the image quality have been examined by considering quality factors such as sharpness, focus and compression. The quality metric is applied after the segmentation process but the quality assessment itself is not expected to be excellent.

Several metrics for iris image quality were developed such as a combination of image and subject covariates, visible light and region-of-interest (ROI).

The combination method measures quality related to motion blur, angular deviation, occlusion and defocus in the quality value of an input iris image, which was developed using near-infra-red-based images suitable for indoor environments.

For an outdoor environment, the visible light under uncontrolled iris image settings is important for finding the differences in the appearance of the acquired iris images (Rathgeb et al., 2012). Methods of evaluating the quality of iris images in visible light are applicable in iris recognition for predicting matching scores.

(Proença, 2006) proposed a metric for the quality assessment of iris images taken in visible light. This metric measures six image quality attributes such as focus score, off-angle score, motion score, occlusion score, iris pigmentation level, and pupil dilation. Later, the impact of image quality is measured on feature matching. The results showed a significant improvement in the iris recognition system by avoiding low-quality images that involved in motion-blur approach (Daugman, 1994). The selected regions of iris images in the most distinguishable changing patterns between the reference iris image and the distorted version execute the feature with quality factors that relate to subject covariates. A correlation between the quality of iris images and performance accuracy is studied based on the quality scores of subject covariates. The iris image quality is assessed locally using a fusion schema at the pixel level using Gaussian Mixture Model (GMM) that presents the probability measure of the quality of local regions in the iris image (Dong et al., 2009). The local quality detects the poorly segmented pixels and removes them from the combination of iris image sequence processes. Even though some of the methods for iris quality assessments are good for near-infrared iris images only a few distortions are acceptable. There are limited distortion types that do not work well for assessing the iris image quality for instance images captured under a visible light environment.

The quality metrics measure the performance accuracy of iris recognition systems. The most crucial parameters are False Acceptance Rate (FAR), False Rejection Rate (FRR) and Equal Error Rate (ERR).

The FAR is the measure of the likelihood that the biometric security system incorrectly accepts access attempted by an unauthorized user. A system's FAR is typically stated as the ratio of the number of false acceptances divided by the number of identification attempts and it is derived as:

(%) FAR = (Number of incidents of false acceptance)/(total number of samples) x 100%

On the other hand, FRR is the measure of the likelihood that the biometric security system incorrectly rejects an access attempt by an authorized user. FRR is considered the most serious of biometric security errors as it gives unauthorized users access to the systems. A system's FRR is typically stated as the ratio of the number of false rejections divided by the number of identification or enrollee attempts and it is defined as:

(%) FRR = (Number of incidents of false rejections)/(total number of samples) x 100%

Equal error rate (EER) is the intersection point at the curve when the FAR line intersects the FRR line, which produces the EER value. As the EER gives lower values in terms of error rates, the value of accuracy is higher.

Another parameter to measure the quality of the iris image is based on Genuine Acceptance Rate (GAR) that measures overall performance accuracy of iris recognition systems. GAR calculates the average score of genuine and fake users but excludes the rejected genuine attempts in the system, which gives the formula, GAR = 1 – FRR. According to genuine and fake accumulation scores given by the recognition system, FRRs and FARs are adjusted by varying values in threshold settings. Figure 10 shows the relationships between FRR, FAR and EER.

Additionally, the performance variations among users give different images belonging to the same person leading to significant differences in the matching scores. The intra-class variability is frequently assigned to the acquisition device or other types of sensors, the controlled or uncontrolled environment and the user condition. A new setting of assessment tools for measuring the performance variations among the iris images is fascinating for developing new algorithms that are robust towards variations and able to improve the performance accuracy of the iris recognition system.

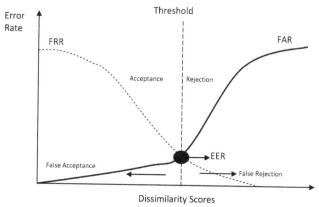

Figure 10: Performance of a Biometric System—Relationship between FAR, FRR and EER.

3.6 SUMMARY

Professor J. Daugman sparked the idea of iris recognition into the biometrics world and it has been commercially used in various industries. The Iris image is transformed into a series of binary formats using circular segmentation, normalization and encoding, called IrisCodes. The stored IrisCodes are compared with real IrisCodes in the matching process to find similar binary bits. However, the IrisCodes produce a mismatch situation when there is a change in the real IrisCode due to occlusions and some lights entering the eye.

The Second Phase of Iris Recognition

The second phase of iris recognition discusses a method for reducing noise and improving the segmentation process for better performance accuracy. Chapter 4 concentrates on short range and long range iris recognition. The short range means the iris image acquisition is less than a meter and only centimeters away from the sensor or camera. Two main methods are applicable in short range type, which are non-circular segmentation and artificial intelligence-based segmentation. The purpose of non-circular and AI segmentation is to overcome the problems existing in circular segmentation in that the shape of the iris is not circular. In fact, AI mimics human behavior and assists the computer in determining the human characteristics for producing an excellent recognition solution. Finding the actual size of iris results in higher accuracy and helps to identify the genuine user. A genuine or fake user is the outcome of iris recognition in a biometric system since organizations use biometrics as the access control system. Organizations are shifting towards industrial revolution and transforming to an autonomous system that involves robots, big data and internet-of-things (IoT). The short range is used for iris detection for entering the building, switching on devices with another level of authentication, and approval in the authentication process in e-commerce transactions. Long range iris recognition is used for longer distances especially for detection at airports, in surveillance CCTVs in local communities and police stations to monitor the safety of the locals.

4.1 OVERVIEW

The objectives of the second phase are to find the unique blob in iris features that sustains for a long time after the enrollment process, exploration of human-approach design for iris recognition, and deployment of iris at-a-distance or on-the-move systems. Studies on investigating the micro-characters of iris texture have gained the attention of researchers using several existing methods for example wavelets and Gabor filters, Cascaded Filter, Ordinal Measures, Multiscale and Feature Selection. An artificial intelligence algorithm is implemented to make the computer mimics human behavior and the iris-at-the distance creates new settings for recognizing the iris, which is further discussed in the following sections. Section 4.2 explains short range distances for iris recognition.

4.2 SHORT RANGE IRIS RECOGNITION

The iris recognition aims to perform the enrolment and comparison processes to produce results that have better image quality and accuracy; present a distinctive user with a lower error rate that leads the genuine to be wrongly recognized as fake; and generates an iris recognition system to be more humanized to detect the iris features intelligently. The iris recognition system is designed based on the unique shape of the iris and only authentic features are captured to be used for the next process which is comparison. There are many techniques to obtain the iris template such as non-circular segmentation and artificial intelligence-based segmentation.

4.2.1 Non-Circular Segmentation

Do you know that the human eye is not perfectly circular? The human eye is not circular and almost oval (Pavan et al., 2012). The urgency of the segmentation process for iris recognition needs to use a non-circular format, that follows the shape of the original iris (Muhammad Arsalan, 2018) exactly which is a mandatory requirement. This is because, with this process, the shape of the iris is located dynamically and it produces higher accuracy during the matching process, especially when the iris image is of high quality. The sample of non-circular formats is shown in Figure 11(a) and (b).

The partial segmentation of iris recognition using the inner boundary of the pupil's circular region increases, and the binary integrated edge intensity curve defeat the difficulties of eyelid occlusions, which are important when a noisy iris image is off angle and blurred. The off-angle and blurred iris textures are due to a non-cooperative imaging environment, with reflections, luminosity, occlusions, and defocus. For non-cooperative environments, a pulling and pushing method is applied in pupil localization as shown in Figure 12(a) and (b).

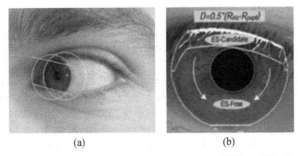

(a)   (b)

Figure 11: (a) Non-Circular Segmentation (Vineet Kumar, 2015) and (b) (Rapaka and Kumar, 2018).

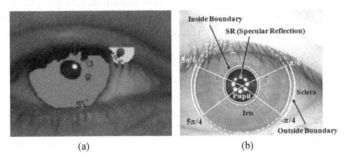

(a)   (b)

Figure 12: Partial Segmentation (a) (Kalavathi, 2016) and (b) (Jamaludin, 2018).

The iris texture development is based on the extraction phase, in which the iris texture is segmented using wavelets and normalized based on Gabor filter techniques.

Based on wavelet techniques, such as Haar, Discrete Cosine Transform (DCT) and Fast Fourier Transform (FFT), the iris features are obtained and represented in real and imaginary fields. The real value presents the information of an iris template meanwhile the imaginary values produce error rate values. Both real and imaginary values produce problems of computer memory consumption and low computational processes.

Another problem with wavelets is that they demand another Gabor filter element to perform normalization. The combination of wavelets and filters results in improved performance especially during matching scores (Minakshi Boruah, 2018) and requires lesser training processes.

However, the combinational way is not suitable for iris images that contain higher error rates, distorted irises, aging and iris images that have occlusions. This is due to difficulties of genuine user detection with the combinational approach.

4.2.1.1 Cascaded Classifiers

Cascaded classifiers provide a technique that constructs a two-stage classification system namely a local feature based classifier (LFC) and global feature classifier (GFC) to measure the inter and intra classes in determining the genuineness (Zhenan Sun et al., 2005). The classifier is based on moment invariants of iris blobs matching which are used to indicate pattern representation of iris features in the extraction and matching phases. The cascaded classifier is different from the typical iris recognition system, which involves phases of data capture, segmentation and normalization, storing and matching that compare a pair of iris features through similarity of iris blocks instead of similarity of pixels in an iris. However, the extraction and matching phases take a low processing time and the accuracy percentage decreases. Nonetheless increase the accuracy performance, another quantization needs to be combined with the classifiers.

4.2.1.2 Ordinal Measures

Ordinal measures extract the encoded qualitative information of a visual signal rather than its quantitative values, which typically involves only additions and subtractions. The application of ordinal measures is suitable for iris recognition on many weak computational platforms such as mobile phones and PDAs as they are not good at multiplication and division. Due to platform limitations, the dissimilarity between two ordinal templates can also be measured by the bitwise XOR operator, which can be easily computed and can be implemented on embedded hardware systems. Furthermore, ordinal measures are developed with multilobe differential filters which consist of short and long filters. To compute flexible intralobe and interlobe parameters such as location, scale, orientation, and distance of the iris template as shown in Figure 13.

The objective of characterizing qualitative relationships between iris regions rather than precise measurements of iris image structures is such that a representation may lose some image-specific information, but it achieves a good trade-off between distinctiveness and robustness. Thus, the trade-off is measured by applying an ordinal measuring technique that evaluates the intrinsic features of iris patterns which are largely invariant to illumination changes. Moreover, compactness and low computational complexity of ordinal measures enable highly efficient iris recognition.

However, the disadvantage of this ordinal measuring technique is that it consumes memory in the database. Additionally, when there is an area in iris features that has been occluded by hair or eyelashes, the crucial information is lost.

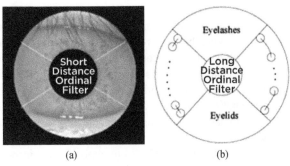

(a)   (b)

Figure 13(a) (b): Ordinal Measures.

4.2.1.3 Multiscale

The blurred iris image is applied with a synthetic blur and it is removed from the blurred image in finding a better quality image (Alaoui, 2013). To produce a better image quality, morphological operations are applied using dilation and erosion which are used to remove the blurriness from the eye image that has eyelashes and eyelids. In the morphological operations, histogram equalization in PCA and DWT is used to get a high contrast iris image that is represented in the fourth column and row.

Moreover, four different databases and the image sizes in each are tested in evaluating the performance in terms of computational cost for there is a pre-processing task. The outcome of the testing shows that the execution time for feature extraction and authentication are the same.

However, the size of a normalized iris image is not the same for each database, yet when the occlusion exists, crucial information is difficult to obtain. Due to the occlusion issue, the feature selection process for selecting only the best feature in the iris template needs to be investigated.

4.2.1.4 Feature Selection

Feature selection is important for choosing a subset of available features by eliminating the unnecessary ones. It is important to get only significant features from the entire texture. Therefore, the feature selection method is used to study iris features to select the best features. The information on iris features obtained is vast and consumes a lot of computational resources. The iris feature selected is based on the best features of the whole iris.

However, this method is unable to identify the best feature selected from among the iris features. The successful detection of the best iris features is up to 30% to 50%. Moreover, the feature selection is implemented through the size reduction of the image matrix with 20×480 pixels, 10×480, and 10×360 pixels in the iris texture which produce good time complexity with better accuracy. Although the algorithm is still vague in finding the most authentic iris features, and it has an advantage, whereby the error rate is decreased to around 50%.

The defocused iris images captured outside the Depth of Field (DOF) of cameras do not rely on special hardware or on computationally expensive image restoration algorithms to exploit the stable bits in the iris code representation. The new algorithm extracts only stable bits which are limited in pattern matching instead of using the entire iris code of representation.

On the other hand, it is a good idea to apply manual inspection for the forensic field, as shown in Figure 14, especially to guarantee the iris features hence it is a tedious task. Moreover, when dealing with huge databases, an autonomous system for human iris recognition helps. None of the foregoing methods conclusively correlate the extracted feature with any specific type of visible feature.

However, since the use of the Hamming Distance measure, the binary features computed with different levels of filters count towards the distance measures with the same weight. The classifier still can only identify strong and weak iris patterns however those detected are still unknown. Based on various iris features, crypts have been used for forensic investigation. The crypts are relatively thin and are observed to be nearly darker than their surroundings (Flynn et al., 2013). However, only 50% accuracy can be achieved using the feature selection method and it is not really precise. For a large number of features, heuristic search is often used to find the best subset of features that measure the score matching between points (Shuai Liu et al., 2018).

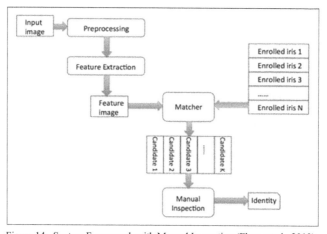

Figure 14: System Framework with Manual Inspection (Flynn et al., 2013).

A lot of efforts have been made to design iris segmentation methods; however, it remains challenging. Studies have shown that the trend of iris segmentation has shifted to artificial intelligence due to the influence from the era of the industrial revolution or IR 4.0.

4.2.2 Artificial Intelligence Based Segmentation and Normalization

The inspiration of artificial intelligence in the iris segmentation and extraction processes is believed to improve a major part of the iris recognition work. Major parts of iris recognition are segmentation and noise removal since both these problems reduce the Boolean decision that brings satisfaction in the search for chromatic spread values about particular chromatic gradients in its neighborhood space. In searching for the chromatic spread values in nearby space faster and accurately, a rapid approach is needed to ensure the speed of iris image processing, called heuristic algorithms (Nicolaie and Valentina, 2010).

Thus, the development of artificial intelligence (AI) algorithms for iris recognition systems give a better outcome in terms of speed, hardware simplicity, accuracy and learning ability. A fast iris segmentation algorithm is based on neural networks (Rahib et al., 2008) and the architecture of the algorithm is provided as:

(C1): Crop the eye image around the pupil.

(C2): Find the pupil centre and pupillary boundary.

(C3): Crop the eye image around the iris.

(C4): Find the iris centre and the limbic boundary.

(C5): Collapse the search space when looking for the pupillary or limbic boundary.

(C6): Identify iris texture occlusions (eyelashes, eyelids, specular lights) if any.

(C7): Encode and match the iris codes.

4.2.2.1 Fuzzy

Computers understand 1 and 0 but not how humans do, since they have their interpretation and varied perceptions. Fuzzy Logic imitates the way of decision making in humans and helps a computer for reasoning inherently vague concepts. Fuzzy logic has a degree of truth that has the scales of measurements that offer a variety of values between 1 and 0. This is important for differentiating the genuine from the non-genuine. It turns out that useful applications of fuzzy logic are not used in high-level artificial intelligence but rather in lower-level machine control.

Fuzzy classifier categorizes behaviour sets of iris features. It has been widely used for iris recognition and has been combined with other algorithms to perform better in accuracy and speed. The purpose of a fuzzy classifier is to identify the iris features more accurately in similarity checks during the recognition phase since the iris template contains high noise. If in image processing, an image that contains high noise means unacceptable to a certain standard, noise in the iris template is part of the relevant information that also needs to be considered. To differentiate the genuine from the non-genuine user, the fuzzy classifier must be able to tolerate noise and learn with the variation in iris template sets. The fuzzy classifier is designed to guarantee that the iris segmentation process gives a similar or better output result than the traditional circular Hough Transform method regardless of the degree of occlusion that varies in each. Here, the pupil and limbic boundary are localized using k-Means run-length encoding technique followed by the iris segmentation process. The fuzzy based iris segmentation performs the outer boundary localization even though the iris boundary should be larger than the size of the pupil boundary. If the pupil boundary is increased, the iris boundary should be reduced for all vital information of the iris contained in between them. In order to control the boundaries, threshold values must be set, since the deduction from the maximum to the minimum pixel grey values is multiplied by 22%. Once the threshold values are set, the pixel values within the threshold are extracted from the left to right positions of the feature space and their recording is aligned with the starting point of the pixel locations. Then, the repeated process produces a stream of pixel values of the iris texture, encoded and saved in the database. In the comparison process, the iris images are compared and pointed to the same position of iris features such as eyelids or eyelashes. The results of the fuzzy based iris recognition have shown an excellent performance accuracy that is 91% with only 1% detection failure and another 8% shows an undefined result. However, the execution time took 7 ½ hours to process 108 users (Saluka Kodituwakku et al., 2008). More research on the speed of computational processing could be further investigated.

A study on iris fuzzy matching with invariant properties found the scheme for two sets of iris feature points adopted in nonlinear normalization providing more accurate position matching (Tsai et al., 2012). The scheme of fuzzy based iris segmentation refined the inner and outer boundaries to obtain a smooth curve. In the extraction phase, the Gabor Filter was applied to detect the local feature points from the segmented iris image in the cartesian coordinate system to generate a rotational-invariant descriptor for each node. A similarity score between two sets of feature points from a pair of iris images was compared and the performance indicated that fuzzy is suitable to detect and recognize the iris characteristics with a high performance accuracy.

4.2.2.2 Genetic Algorithm

A genetic algorithm is a mathematical formulation based on DNA chromosomes that show evolution for obtaining an optimal solution. The chromosomes contain a set of populations, which are called genes, and they store a set of varied information about the gene type. To know how good the solution is by identifying the scale of determination in the fitness value, and the fitness score shows the variations of executing the population on the fitness value. This is typically implemented in the fitness function. The fitness value is dependent on cases, which differ from one another. Genetic Algorithm helps the biometric field to learn the epigenetic variance inside the human iris for higher accuracy and better recognition performance.

Genetic algorithms are an approach to optimization and learning based loosely on principles of biological evolution, which are simple to construct, and their implementation does not require a large amount of storage, making them a sufficient choice for an optimization problem. Optimal scheduling is a nonlinear problem that cannot be solved easily as yet. A Genetic Algorithm could serve to find a decent solution in a limited amount of time. Genetic algorithms are inspired by Darwin's theory of evolution "survival of fittest". It searches the solution space of a function through the use of simulated evolution (survival of the fittest) strategy. Generally, the fittest individuals of any population have a greater chance to reproduce and survive, to the next generation. Thus it contributes to improving successive generations. However, inferior individuals can survive by chance and also reproduce. Genetic algorithms have been shown to solve linear and nonlinear problems by exploring all regions of the state space and exponentially exploiting promising areas through the application of mutation, crossover and selection operations to individuals in the population. It integrates numerical analysis, matrix computation and graphics in an easy-to-use environment. Therefore, these functions can be re-implemented from one hardware architecture to another without even a recompilation step. The Genetic Algorithms are used to optimize the biometric comparator using the Hamming Distance (Urashveen Kour, 2019). Furthermore, the false acceptance and rejection rates are minimized in recognition; and the size of the features subset selected is reduced.

The benefit of a Genetic Algorithm is that it overcomes the problem, for example, by scaling and performing sensitivity towards the weights in selecting the optimal features in the feature space. To simulate the process of evolution, the selected chromosomes experience genetic operations, such as crossover and mutation. Each individual of the current population is tested based on the fitness function. The extracted iris features by Genetic Algorithms form a collection of candidate features called feature pools. Thus, the fitness function increases the efficiency and effectiveness of the evolutionary search. Based on the new fitness function and the feature selection method recognition accuracy increases and reduces the feature dimension. The feature selection technique with the new fitness function reduces the FAR and FRR significantly which are capable of making the more efficient and effective classifications. Moreover, the genetic algorithm-based feature selection and information feature space improve the analysis of iris data.

4.2.2.3 Artificial Neural Networks (ANNs)

The ANN or in short called Neural Network (NN) mimics how the brain works. These computing systems are vaguely inspired by the biological neural networks that constitute animal brains. An ANN is based on a collection of connected units or nodes called artificial neurons, in which the outputs of the artificial neurons are an input to another set of artificial neurons. Each node represents an artificial neuron and an arrow to indicate the connection of the input to output.

The goal of ANN is to instruct the computer to think like a human brain in recognizing an object. In this case, the ANN is adopted to identify the human iris template. The ANN helps the computer to understand humans by thinking like a human. ANNs have given marvelous outcomes in many applications such as classification and categorization, prediction, pattern recognition and control. An artificial neural network comprises an interrelated group of artificial neurons. For instance, a network performs computation and deploys information based on the connectionist approach in a similar but simpler pattern than the brain executes.

Five Artificial Neural Network (ANN) models have been studied separately, (a) feed forward (FFBPNN), (b) cascade forward (CFBPNN), (c) function fitting (FitNet), (d) pattern recognition (PatternNet) and (e) learning vector quantization (LVQNet). For each ANN model, two architectures were constructed separately; 4 layers and 7 layers, each with different numbers of hidden layer units (5, 10 and 15). Ten different ANN optimization training algorithms (LM, BFG, BR, CGF, GD, GDM, GDA, GDX, OSS and RP) were used to train each model separately. Experiments were conducted for each one of the five models. Each model used two different architectures, a different number of hidden layer neurons and ten different training algorithms. The performance results of the models were compared according to mean square error to identify the best ANN model. The results showed that the PatternNet model was the best model used. A comparison between the ten training algorithms was performed with the PatternNet model. Comparison results showed that TrainLM was the best training algorithm for the iris recognition system (Omaima et al., 2012). The most popular ANN is the Multi-Layer Perceptron (MLP) where neurons in a feedforward type network perform a biased weighted averaging of their inputs and this sum is then subjected to a transfer function, to limit the output value (Fadi et al., 2011).

A new technique employing both eyes of an individual is implemented and tested using the ANN (MahaSharkas, 2016). The feature vector is generated in several ways either by using the approximation coefficients directly or dividing the approximation image into 8×8 blocks in the case of the 1st level and 4×4 blocks in the case of the second level and taking the mean to generate the feature vector. Training and testing are done in several ways too. The best feature vectors were the ones generated from taking the mean. They were of size 184 or 96 coefficients where training was performed with data from the left and right eyes. Testing was done with data from either eye. It could be said that the second level is better as the length of the feature vector is smaller. The novelty of this technique is that it suggests that data of the right or left eye can be used for personal identification with no limitations. This helps personnel suffering from illness or discomfort in either eye. Also combining information from both eyes can help improve the recognition rate (MahaSharkas, 2016).

4.2.2.4 Deep Learning

Deep learning is a machine learning technique that instructs the computer to mimic human behaviour since it uses neural networks to learn about human abilities. Computers understand zero and ones but a human interprets things through feelings and perceptions. The deep learning algorithm assists the computer to learn like a human does and assists decision making in daily processes and critical planning.

Iris segmentation is a critical step in the entire iris recognition process. In neural networks, Region Based Convolutional Neural Networks (R-CNN) have been used for object detection and locating points in an image. The R-CNN does a Selective Search to find the important point in the Region of Interest (ROI) and the Support Vector Machine (SVM) classifier determines the feature object inside each of the ROI spaces. A combination method of learning-based and edge-based algorithms for iris segmentation is implemented using Faster R-CNN with only six layers and is built to locate and classify the eye (Li Yung-Hui et al.,

2019). The bounding box found by Faster R-CNN, and the pupillary region is located using a Gaussian mixture model. The circular boundary of the pupillary region is fit according to five key boundary points. A boundary point selection algorithm is used to find the boundary points of the limbus, and its circular boundary is constructed using these boundary points. Experimental results show that the proposed iris segmentation method achieves 95.49% accuracy with the challenging CASIA (Li Yung-Hui et al., 2019).

In an iris image, most of the iris textures are concentrated in the iris region close to the pupillary boundary. If the boundary of the pupillary region is not accurately located, a large number of iris textures are missed in the feature extraction step. In most cases, the limbus boundary is obscured by eyelashes, eyelids, and specular reflections, and thus, a number of noisy features are extracted in the feature extraction step, if the limbus boundary is not accurately located in the iris segmentation step.

4.2.2.5 Harmony

Harmony is a series of single melodies that creates wonderful music to listen to. The use of Harmony Search Algorithm (HSA) is successfully used in areas such as function optimization, mechanical structure design, pipe network optimization and optimizing the classification systems. The HSA is inspired by the musical performance process. When musicians compose a harmony, they usually try various possible combinations of pitches stored in their memory. This search for perfect harmony is indeed analogous to the procedure of finding the optimal solutions to engineering problems. The HSA method is inspired by the working principles of harmony improvisation consisting of three operators: random search, harmony memory considering rule, and pitch adjusting rule. HSA searches the unique iris template based on several arrangements for finding the best feature. The ways of handling exploration and exploitation with the three operators make the HSA a unique metaheuristic algorithm (Sivakamasundari, 2019).

4.3 LONG RANGE IRIS RECOGNITION

The initial application of iris recognition systems required the image of the user's eye to be captured within a short distance range from the sensor and it was a rigid acquisition process for obtaining a high-quality image. For making iris recognition more convenient for use by the community, a longer distance range for iris detection could be beneficial for several applications in domains such as border control, surveillance, law enforcement, industrial services and military.

The border control system has been widely used in several airports across the world in countries such as Canada and United Kingdom. It scans passengers and employees to detect whether the person is real or fake before allowing access to the system.

The surveillance system monitors the pedestrian and movement of typical people who pass by the area for routine activities. The purpose of monitoring the behaviour of the crowd and the place is to protect them. There has been an increasing interest in developing automated surveillance applications, using biometrics especially.

Prevention of crime and security applications are implemented through Law Enforcement. Potentially, they can enhance the safety of both citizens and law enforcement officials.

Industrial Service improves user convenience in the service industry (e.g., banks, retail stores, casinos, etc.). A sample application includes identifying shoppers as they enter a store to provide them with customized sales (assuming relaxed social and privacy concerns).

The Military used a hand-held iris recognition device to ensure a high level of cooperation from participants that could significantly advance monitoring, tracking, and identification without imposing many restrictions.

4.3.1 Iris Detection at-a-Distance (IAAD) Framework

Iris Detection at-a-Distance (IAAD) framework is generally used to identify the person in most of the applications. The system is considered to be a significant innovation in iris recognition at a distance. The setup is often known by its commercial name "Iris On the Move" (IOM), popularized by the Sarnoff Corporation. Owing to the drastic improvement in user convenience, it is often considered as the first, fully operational, remote iris recognition system. The system captures irises from a moving subject situated at a distance from the camera. In this system, different features of the iris image are extracted in addition to enhancing its superiority. Throughout times various structures have been used to design and finish iris affirmation systems, which work at a longer separation range from one meter to sixty meters. Because of such a large scope of iris detection schemes in addition iris attainment schemes provide the best applications to the client. The iris at a distance involves iris recognition between a radius range of 1 to 30 meters. Iris features are detected by the sensor from longer distances. This approach is used at airports for the prevention of pandemics such as COVID-19 and other diseases.

Figure 15 shows that the position of the sensor is fixed, and the users are required to walk along with a guideline and look directly at the camera. Users are required to pass through a portal with a moderate level of cooperation: looking forward, walking at a normal pace, and not engaging in behaviour intended to prevent iris image acquisition.

The evolution of IAAD techniques started with IOM that uses a commercial off-the-shelf Pulnix TM-40 0 0CL sensor with a resolution of 2048 × 2048 pixels, capable of capturing 15 frames per second. The image capturing volume is about 20 cm wide × 40 cm high × 10 cm deep at a distance of approximately 3 m from the sensor. The setup could be extended by adding additional sensors to increase the coverage area (Kien Nguyen, 2017). Illumination is provided by 8 strobed illuminators with high-power Light Emitting Diodes (LEDs). These LEDs are synchronized with the camera through an embedded circuit. The identification accuracy is evaluated using test data corresponding to 119 subjects, and reported to be 99% when the participants were trained on the acquisition protocol. However, the corresponding accuracy involving untrained participants was reported to be 78%. The performance of an IOM system is impeded by three factors. First, because of its small capturing volume, it cannot capture irises of people with varying heights. Second, the users are expected to be cooperative by not engaging in behaviour intended to prevent iris image acquisition. Third, specular reflections in irises and eyeglasses caused by using a large number of illuminators (8) reduce the recognition accuracy.

Another attempt at IAAD was carried out by De Villar, to recognize the irises from a 30 m distance (De Villar et al., 2010). A WFoV 1392 × 1024 camera with a 75 mm lens was employed to detect the face and eyes. Subsequently, a NFoV 2592 × 1944 73.5-fps camera with a pixel

Figure 15: The Iris Detection at-a-Distance System (Nguyen et al., 2017).

size of 2.2 microns was used to capture irises. A Meade LX200-R F/10 8 inches reflecting telescope attached to the camera was used to capture the iris at a 190-pixel resolution. This telescope was primarily designed for observing stars and other stellar objects in space. In order to reduce the focus distance from infinity to 30 m, an 18-centimeter-extension tube was used between the camera and eyepiece. The NFoV camera and the telescope are mounted on a PTU, which is controlled by the location of the eyes as detected by the WFoV camera. A range finder providing an estimate of the subject's standoff distance is mounted on the telescope to enable automatic focusing. The estimate has been reported to be highly accurate, with a margin of error of around 1 cm.

Iris recognition is a powerful biometric for personal identification, but it is difficult to acquire good-quality iris images in real time. For making iris recognition more convenient to use, Wenbo Dong designed an iris recognition system functional at a distance of about 3 meters. There are many key issues in designing such a system, including iris image acquisition, human-machine-interface and image processing. In this paper, we introduce how to deal with these problems and accomplish the engineering design respectively. Experiments show that the system is convenient to use at a distance of 3 meters and the recognition rate is not worse than the state-of-the-art close-range systems (Wenbo Dong et al., 2009). The technology uses an artificial intelligence algorithm to self-adapt to adjust to the height of a person and locate the eye on the facial expression. Figure 16 shows the iris-at-the-distance platform proposed by (Wenbo Dong et al., 2009).

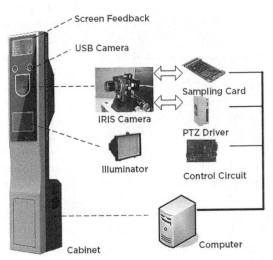

Figure16: The Platform of Iris-at-a-Distance (Wenbo Dong et al., 2009).

4.4 CHALLENGES IN SECOND PHASE OF IRIS RECOGNITION

The early phase of iris recognition faced a high noise rate in iris images and circular segmentation. The second phase explains various problems occurring at different stages of iris recognition such as pre-processing, feature extraction, template matching, sensors and security of the iris template.

4.4.1 Pre-processing

The Iris is a muscle-filled organ (trabeculae), and the contraction and dilation movements distort more and more of its pseudo-circumference (Gonzaga et al., 2009). Collectively, the pre-processing of images is a lengthy stage and therefore, difficult to perform manually. The automatic procedure always uses the same naming sequences at different stages of processing. In case one disastrous problem occurs it may permanently affect the sequences of the input images. The second part in the pre-processing of the iris image is the image quality evaluation. In practice, the quality of some iris images is so terrible that error matching occurs (Lei et al., 2003). Image quality assessment plays an important role in automated biometric systems for two reasons, (1) system performance (recognition and segmentation), and (2) interoperability. Low quality images have poor lighting defocus blur, off-angle, and heavy occlusion, which have a negative impact on even the best available segmentation algorithms (Kalka et al., 2006). Pre-processing includes processes of iris normalization, iris image enhancement and denoising. Irises of different people may be captured in different sizes; also, the size of the iris of the same person may change because of the variation in illumination. Such elastic deformations in iris texture affect the results of iris matching. Normalization involves the process of organizing data to minimize redundancy and then dividing the database into two or more tables and defining relationships between the tables. The problems related to normalization are that the image has low contrast and may have non-uniform illumination caused by the position of light sources. The concept of image enhancement using histogram equalization and removal of noise by filtering the image with a low pass Gaussian Filter produces a better quality image. The problem with histogram equalization is it produces undesirable effects when applied to images with low colour depth (bits per pixel). For example, if applied to an 8-bit image displayed with an 8-bit grey scale it further reduces colour depth (number of unique shades of grey) of the image. Histogram equalization works the best when applied to images with much higher colour depth than palette size, like continuous data or 16-bit grayscale images (Moorthi et al., 2010).

Proenca et al. (2006) evaluated four different clustering algorithms for pre-processing the images to enhance contrast. The fuzzy k-means clustering algorithm used on the position and intensity feature vector was found to be best compared with Daugman (1994) algorithms. The algorithm for pre-processing is tested on the UBIRIS dataset, which contains one session of high-quality images, and another dataset of lower-quality images. The algorithm by Proenca et al. (2006) performed with 98.02% accuracy on the good dataset, but with a degraded performance of 97.88% accuracy on the poorer quality dataset.

Denoising is done using either the mean filter or median filter. The main problem with the mean filter is that a single pixel with a very unrepresentative value affects the mean value of all the pixels in its neighbourhood. When the filter neighbourhood spans an edge, the filter interpolates new values for pixels on the edge and makes it blurred at that edge. This is the biggest problem when a sharp-edged image is required in the output. This problem is removed by the median filter. The median filter is often a better filter for reducing noise than the mean filter, but it takes a longer time to compute.

4.4.2 Feature Extraction

Iris feature extraction is a process of obtaining the information from a two-dimensional image in deciding whether the individual is the real user or not in the matching phase based on quality metrics.

One of the problems in feature-based iris recognition is that the matching performance is significantly influenced by many parameters in the feature extraction process, which may vary depending on environmental factors of image acquisition (Miyazawa et al., 2005). The human eye is sensitive to visible light. The pupil contracts and dilates under the effect of the visible light, and the iris and the sclera exceptionally reflect within this range.

Another problem is to capture an image of the human iris by using visible light without destroying the quality of the iris image. The NIR illumination generates good resolution and definition images. However, since they are not "visible" to the human eye, they do not allow for the necessary stimuli for the pupil to perform contraction and dilation movements. The image quality is compromised, thus making the extraction of features difficult (Gonzaga et al., 2009). These images do not provide enough quality for dependable biometric recognition.

Designing iris recognition systems could be viewed as a heuristic way of solving a satisfactory constraint problem. The challenge in iris recognition is to design an exploratory supervised intelligent agent enabled to evolve itself, control the complex computations and validate it. Moreover, the problem of computational processing consumes a lot of energy and it takes long hours to execute programming functions. Huge memory allocation is needed for compilation and execution in the computing process.

There is no separation between the class of matching scores and non-matching scores (the classes are intricate and their separation is fuzzy because some similarity values can be obtained both as matching and non-matching scores) (Nicolaie and Valentina, 2010).

Quality of iris images is quantified as a matter of degree since the majority of the best approaches for iris recognition using binary iris codes retrieve phase information from the iris texture and compare the Hamming Distance between iris codes for a recognition threshold. One of the most recent proprietary iris code formats, is owned by Daugman and tested by NIST (George et al., 2019). The quality of an iris recognition system is very often expressed through the False Rejection and Acceptance Rates (FRR and FAR) which illustrate the relationship between user comfort and the risk of allowing identity confusion. A successful match result is dependent on the average quality of the eye images used. There is no solid reason for the neural approaches for iris encoding and matching usually not achieving the same performance. In terms of artificial intelligence, neural network architecture or a heuristic algorithm is able to replicate currently available iris recognition results obtained by comparing the iris codes directly. Such an approach assumes that each enrolled identity is stored as a trained memory or as a feature vector and will be able to classify iris codes as well by possibly preserving the quality of the separation between genuine and imposter score distributions in terms of False Acceptance or Rejection Rates (Nicolaie and Valentina, 2010).

4.4.3 Template Matching

Template matching involved the formal verification or identification of iris recognition but failed due to the fact that instead of comparing two normalized iris images (two matrices of unsigned 8-bit integers) directly, the similarity between two 'shadows' left by them in a space of binary matrices was tested. Hence, finding two different irises such that their codes match each other is just a matter of time and chance. Such a counter-example was already found during a study concerning long-term evolutions on the currency exchange global market (Nicolaie and Valentina, 2010).

The template is compared with the other templates stored in a database until either a matching template is found and the person is identified, or no match is found and the person remains unidentified. The matching process can be done by the use of an image pyramid. This is a series of images, at different scales, which are formed by repeatedly filtering and sub-sampling the original image to generate a sequence of reduced resolution images. More than one template having different scales and rotations, using a single template decreases the accuracy, which improves the execution speed for image comparison. However, the computation time still scales linearly with the size of the set.

4.4.4 Sensors

The success of the iris image captured is highly dependent upon the quality of the image captured by the sensor. If the image is of low quality and contains random specular reflections in and around the iris, the performance of iris recognition is degraded (Hanna et al., 1996) developed a system that would actively find the eye of the nearest user who stood between 1 and 3 feet from the cameras. Their system used two wide field-of-view cameras and a cross-correlation-based stereo algorithm to search for the coarse location of the head. They used a template-based method to search for the characteristic arrangements of features in the face. Then, a narrow field-of-view (NFOV) camera would confirm the presence of the eye and acquired the eye image. Two incandescent lights, one on each side of the camera, illuminated the face. The NFOV camera eye-finding algorithm searched for the specular reflections of these lights to locate the eye.

To overcome the problem of blurred images a CCD sensor in interlaced scan mode, and a frame are combined by two fields with an interval of 20 ms or less, and the resulting image involves obvious interlacing lines in the horizontal direction (Ma et al., 2002). Bachoo et al. (2005) approach the detection of eyelash occlusions using the gray-level co-occurrence matrix (GLCM) pattern analysis technique. Possible challenges for this approach are choosing the correct window size and dealing with windows that have a mixture of types.

Most iris recognition devices are capable of capturing only one image of an iris at a time. After each image capture, the device user must manually enter several pieces of identifying information, including whether the image is of a left eye or a right eye. Hence, the single capturing ability of iris recognition devices slows the data collection process and increases the likelihood that they are misidentified.

Even when a good quality camera is used, the result is commonly useless for iris recognition. Autofocus, if applied, usually concentrates on the face not on the iris itself, but when auto-focus is disabled then the distance between the head and the camera must be kept stable, fixed manually by the camera operator or by the user himself. This kind of acquisition reduces image quality, and is very uncomfortable for the user (Lorenz et al., 2008).

4.4.5 Iris Template Security

Biometrics is better than passwords when it comes to security, but they are not fool-proof. The next time you log into your bank account to pay a bill, instead of entering your password, you might have to take a picture of your eye to gain access. Welcome to the world of biometric authentication, where your eyes, ears, and fingerprints are the access code to prove individual identity. Biometric technology becomes commonplace sooner rather than later (Subha et al., 2019). Despite the benefits, some flaws still must be addressed. Here are three major issues facing biometric security:

1: Biometrics is not private:

Biometrics seem secure but that does not mean they are more secure than passwords. A password is inherently private because you are the only one who knows it. Hackers acquire it by brute force attacks or phishing, but generally, people cannot access it. On the other hand, biometrics are inherently public. Think about it: your ears, eyes, and face are exposed. You reveal your eyes whenever you look at things. With fingerprint recognition you leave fingerprints everywhere you go. With voice recognition, someone is recording your voice. Essentially, there is easy access to all identifiers. Your image is stored in more places than you realize. Not only does Facebook recognize your face, but every store you visit records and saves your image in its database to identify you and analyze your buying habits. Law enforcement agencies nation wide can store your image without consent. The problem is identity management and security. Personal identifiable information (PII) needs to have access control in place to prevent identity theft. All it takes is for a hacker to breach any of those databases to leak and steal your biometric identification.

2: Biometrics are Hackable

Once hackers have a picture of someone's ear, eye, or finger, they can easily gain access to their accounts. The hacker obtains high-resolution photos of the politician's thumb from press conferences and reconstructs the thumbprint using VeriFinger software. If you think an eye scan may be more secure, think again. Hackers fooled the Samsung S8 iris recognition system by placing a contact lens over a photo of a user's eye. However, it was not a high-priced hack either.

3: Biometric Hacks May Have Greater Consequences

Since a biometric reveals part of a user's identity, if stolen, it can be used to falsify legal documents, passports, or criminal records, which can do more damage than a stolen credit card number. Biometrics may be the security measure of the future, but it isn't time to discard your passwords yet. Biometrics provide another level of security, but they are not fool proof.

4.5 SUMMARY

The second phase of iris recognition offers a system with more user-friendliness, effectiveness, efficiency, and higher performance accuracy in biometric systems. Additionally, the method of implementation for iris recognition covers short-range and long-range detection. The short-range method consists of non-circular segmentation techniques such as cascaded, multiscale, partial segmentation, feature selection and artificial intelligence that give an alternative approach for segmentation to achieve a better performance accuracy. The purpose of the short-range iris detection is to obtain iris templates with a good quality image and solely information about the iris template. Meanwhile, the long-range method emphasis is on the deployment of iris at-a-distance or on-the-move systems in CCTVs for application in border control, airport systems and video surveillance systems. Moreover, long-range detection helps the enforcement to control and monitor the citizens in the areas prone to crimes and dangerous activities.

Swarm-Inspired Iris Recognition

Chapter 5 illustrates the algorithm and findings of swarm intelligence for iris recognition. Two main algorithms have been discussed in this chapter, which is ant colony optimization (ACO) and particle swarm optimization (PSO) applied to iris recognition. The concept and mechanism of each algorithm are explained. Iris recognition is developed using ACO and PSO due to their adaptability in searching for unique features inside the iris. The optimization criteria give the biometric system a better noise tolerance and detection.

5.1 OVERVIEW

Swarm intelligence in nature-inspired computing contributes an optimization solution for a day-to-day problem. The applications of swarm intelligence change ordinary lives to be extraordinary, easy, and more manageable (Capizzi et al., 2015), (Bonanno et al., 2013). For example, routine activities using robots for giving the recommendation of choices (Shi et al., 2016), voice assistants for messaging (Polap, 2019), image recognition (Zoph et al., 2018) and autopilot mode for driving selection (Farjadian et al., 2018). Progressively, the intelligence machine takes charge of daily operations due to its autonomous capabilities, performance efficiency, effectiveness and high accuracy. In fact, heuristics capability, self-learning ability, optimization in computational processes, fast response and noise tolerance are other reasons for swarm intelligence applications in the real world and making the industry 4.0 era a reality.

Studies have shown increasing numbers in the use of swarm intelligence algorithms in biometric systems (Santosh Kumar et al., 2015), (Salima Nebti and Abdallah Boukerram, 2016), (Sajid Ali Khan et al., 2018) and (Abhishek P. Iyer et al., 2020). The implementation of biometrics using swarm intelligence algorithms involves various kinds of human traits such as faces (Aneesh et al., 2011), iris (Lin et al., 2009), fingerprints (Ching-Tang Hsieh and Chia-Shing Hu, 2014), ears (Lamis Ghoualmi, 2016), fireflies (Daniela Sánchez et al., 2017) and electrocardiograms (ECG) (Kiran et al., 2019). The reason that pushes biometric systems to use swarm intelligence is the minimal space required for biometric features development (Khudher and Ibrahim, 2020), fewer metrics for measurements and the capability to handle images with a high noise rate. The noise rate occurs in the human iris due to changes inside the features of the iris itself because of several factors such as aging, medical surgery and health conditions. Where the iris template deviates from the original data, especially during the verification process.

The current technology of iris recognition during matching is not able to recognize the real user in reality especially when the real user ages and has undergone medical surgery due to a cataract or some other illness. Moreover, the current methods focus on the encoding process that involves various techniques transforming iris templates into iris codes called machine-based learning. In fact, in many situations during pandemics and an industrial revolution situation, most industries such as transportation, communication, industrial production and administration changed their way of working towards autonomous, pervasive device orientation that is more self-configuring in the future.

Thus, the iris recognition system needs a new system that is based on a human approach development, which is more humanized to determine the natural features for iris detection and recognition. A human approach system means the use of natural computing for iris recognition development that involves DNA computing, quantum computing and bio-computing for detecting the unique characteristics based on features. Swarm intelligence falls under the bio-computing field that has inspiration, identification and application features. The goal is to obtain optimization and robustness in performance. Furthermore, self-organized control and cooperation (decentralized), indirect interactions and distributed task allocations are the expected criteria of the natural behaviours for future iris recognition systems. Self-organization is a set of dynamical mechanism structures that appear at the global level of a system from the interactions of its lower-level components. There are five bases of self-organization namely feedback (positive and negative), randomness, errors, random walks and multiple interactions. Meanwhile, indirect interactions mean a collaboration of universal coordination called "stigmergy" in dynamic environments for interactions and information updates by using signals and landmarks. A better understanding of stigmergy mechanisms is agents (for example artificial ants) leaving behind traces within an environment from one point to another for future simulation action. A combination of positive and negative feedbacks improves the looping actions that enhance the mutual understanding between agents without the need for planning, control and direct communication. Over time, the decentralized control scheme takes charge to perform self-awareness and organizing in information sharing until the system stabilises. The distributed task allocation is an algorithm for determining an instantaneous probabilistic optimal policy for task allocation. The policy is independent of the state of the system and thus does not require information exchange among the agents during task performance.

In iris recognition, the application of swarm intelligence has found solutions to hard computational problems and produces social insects in computational operations. A metaheuristic-based iris recognition includes four phases, which are pre-processing, extraction, feature selection, and classification (Mithuna, 2017).

The segmentation and normalization process starts with the pupil and iris boundaries. They are localized and the process of contouring starts from the inner to the outer, iris called segmentation. Typically, circular iris segmentation and normalization involve the Hough Transform and Integral Daugman Operator method, in which the iris images are segmented and the entire iris texture is nomalized into a rectangular shape, regardless of the presence of noise (eyelids, eyelashes, and occlusions) since it represents the person's vital information. The pre-processing phase turns the iris image into order to find effective regions for extracting features. The Harris corner detection method is used to locate and segment the human eye areas (Trujillo et al., 2005). Then, the iris location algorithm based on improved calculus operators is used to find the iris region. After the iris region is segmented and normalized, the pre-processing is complete. The upper half of the whole circular iris region is greatly affected by the eyelids and eyelashes. To avoid their interference with the iris texture, only features from the lower half of the circular region are extracted (Zhang et al., 2018).

Feature extraction focuses on the method of Gabor filters. The operation is suitable for human visual processing, and has the advantage of being parameterizable in terms of frequency and orientation. Gabor filters are applicable to various images. The Gabor function associates a Gaussian curve and an oriented sinusoid in image processing, which works in a two dimensional space domain.

$$G\,(x,\,y,\,\theta,\,f) = e^{-\dfrac{1}{2}\left(\dfrac{x_\theta^2}{\sigma_x^2} + \dfrac{y_\theta^2}{\sigma_y^2}\right)}\cos\,(2\pi fx\theta)$$

where, $x_\theta = x\cos\theta + y\sin\theta$ and $y_\theta = y\cos\theta - x\sin\theta$

The orientation of the sinusoid, frequency and the standard deviation of the Gaussian is along the coordinate axis. Applying this function to a convolution mask, the convolution filter is called a Gabor filter, $f = \frac{\sqrt{2}}{10}$ and $\sigma_x = \sigma_y = 7$.

The application of a Gabor filter, g, mask, M, radius r of an image, I, width m, and height, n, is summarized as:

$$g\,(I) = J = M \times I$$

where J is the matrix of dimension $m \times n$ and for i, j $\in$ 1,2,3 ... , $r \le i < m - r$ and $r \le j < n - r$

$$J_{i,j} = \Sigma_{k=-r}^{r}\Sigma_{l=-r}^{k} M_{k,l} \times I_{(i-k),(j-l)}$$
$$= \Sigma_{k=-r}^{r}\Sigma_{l=-r}^{r} G(k,l,\theta,f) \times I_{(i-k),(j-l)}$$

Gabor filters produce a possible isolation between the contours of an image orientation perpendicular to θ, and corresponding to a certain thickness that depends on f.

Feature extraction by Wavelet Moments is represented by the input image itself with reduced size, known as an approximation coefficient. However, the detailed coefficients are referred to as; diagonal (d), horizontal (h) and vertical (v). The outcome of first level DWT on an image is represented as:

$$M = M_a^1 + \{M_h^1 + M_v^1 + M_d^1\}$$

Dimension reduction of input data is achieved using N-level DWT. After 4-level DWT, the image M is expressed as:

$$M = M_a^4 + \Sigma_{i=1}^{4}\left\{\{M_h^i + M_v^i + M_d^i\}\right\}$$

After 2-level DWT, input image having the dimension m x n is estimated to $\frac{m}{2} \times \frac{n}{2}$. Fourier transform is applied to get the frequency domain image that is expressed as:

$$DWT_{x(n)} = \begin{cases} dd_{j,k} = \Sigma img(n)hh*_s\,(n-2^s r) \\ ap_{j,k} = \Sigma img(n)ll*_s\,(n-2^s r) \end{cases}$$

where, $ap_{j,k}$ are the approximate coefficients and $dd_{j,k}$ are the detailed coefficients.

Functions are low pass and high pass filters respectively. Parameters are wavelet translations and scale factors respectively. The Standard deviation and the mean are given by the mean of a random variable vector, having scalar observations, expressed as:

$$\mu_{mn} = \frac{1}{N} \Sigma_{i,j=1}^{N} ap_{ij},$$

where the approximate coefficient is symbolized by ap_{ij}, and the standard deviation is:

$$\sigma_{mn} = \sqrt{\frac{\Sigma_{i=1}^{m}\Sigma_{j=1}^{n}(|I_{mn}(i,j)|\mu_{mn})^2}{N-1}}$$

where $I_{mn}(i, j)$ shows the value detected by the sample items. With the use of mean and standard deviation, the wavelet moments are expressed as:

$$f_g = (\mu_{00}, \sigma_{00}, \mu_{01}, \sigma_{01} \ldots \ldots \mu_{45}, \sigma_{45}).$$

Studies on feature selection of the iris texture from its original structure have gained attention from some researchers (Yoon, 2005), (Proença et al., 2006), (Chen et al., 2007), (Sun and Tan, 2009), (Han et al., 2010), (Rajan et al., 2012) and (Sharma et al., 2013) hence, it is vital for choosing a unique feature by eliminating the unnecessary ones since the iris feature information obtained can be tremendously huge and consequently consumes a lot of computational resources (Garg et al., 2012). Therefore, the unique iris feature selected is based on the best feature points from the entire iris texture, which is required in determining the changes or instability in iris texture intelligently. Biometric iris recognition has been successfully employed in interactions with the society and with computers. A novel iris biometric system is proposed with the exploitation of swarm-based feature selection methods such as PSO and ACO.

In swarm intelligence, particle swarm optimization (PSO) and ant colony optimization (ACO) are the most used nature-inspired algorithms to solve optimization problems. Swarm algorithms are chosen based on their winning criteria. Two of the most prominent criteria that make them preferred algorithms are that they are able to search elements using the stimergy mechanism and achieve faster computational time compared with other nature inspired computational algorithms.

ACO is used to select the best iris feature from the iris texture. The advantages of ACO compared to PSO are; it intelligently handles noise better than PSO, which gives good PSNR values, accurate detection of unique features in iris recognition, and faster encoding time (June et al., 2011).

However, the disadvantage of ACO is that, it takes a longer time in iteration to converge to optimal solutions due to random movements of the artificial ants. In order to stop the iteration of movement, a target needs to be initialized for ants to start searching for unique iris features and end the process after meeting the target value. The ACO method has been combined with the Content based Image Retrieval (CBIR) field to develop a new approach. The reason ACO being applicable in various fields is that natural computing assists in solving many problems like approximation for searching solutions, discrete optimization problems, pattern recognition and image processing. Moreover, the capability of artificial ants to perform monitoring and synchronization to find solutions to optimization problems shows a remarkable representation.

Feature selection consists of univariate, recursive elimination. L1 based and tree-based methods establish ways to select only 50% of the iris texture features for processing. The rest of them are eventually removed from the iris template. On the other hand, bio-inspired heuristic optimization algorithms, such as ACO and PSO, are found promising for selecting more than 50% of the best features from the entire iris texture. Therefore, it was decided that the best method to adopt for investigation is to adapt bio-inspired feature selection into the extraction process.

PSO and ACO are currently two common techniques in bio-inspired feature selection used to create iris templates in biometric recognition systems. PSO and ACO are both metaheuristic methods that have been widely used to solve different types of optimization problems. The main idea of ACO is to model the problem as the search for a minimum cost path in a graph using artificial ants. Each ant has a rather simple behaviour so that it finds only poor-quality paths on its own. Better paths are found as the emergent result of the overall cooperation among ants in the colony. This cooperation is performed indirect way through pheromone laying. Likewise, PSO is a population-based search procedure in which an individual particle adjusts its position according to its own experience, and the experience of the fittest neighbouring particle. It optimizes a problem by iteratively trying to improve a candidate solution with regards to a given quality measure.

A considerable amount of literature has been published on bio-inspired feature selection which involves heuristic or random search to reduce the FRR and computing time. The goal of bio-inspired feature selection is to reduce the dimensionality of the feature space, limit storage requirements, remove the redundant, speed up the computational time of the learning algorithms, data quality improvement, performance enhancement and increasing the accuracy of the resulting approach (Ladha et al., 2011). Authentic iris features (Ma et al., 2009) have been discovered using ACO (Sharma et al., 2013) and PSO (Logannathan, 2012), (Ghodrati et al., 2011), (Chen et al., 2014) for better recognition and classification. In fact, they are useful algorithms due to their capabilities for solving nonlinear and well-constrained problems (Rai et al., 2013) and useful in finding unique features (crypts, furrows, pigment blotches, and collarettes) in the iris texture.

The classification method in swarm-based iris recognition is still using the machine learning technique such as SVM, Random Forest, decision trees and boosted trees to perform the categorization of unique iris features. Most of these machine learning techniques are combined with the metaheuristic techniques for boosting the performance. Moreover, metaheuristic approaches are concerned with searching the path to be followed or how memory is to be exploited. For a formal classification of local search algorithms based on an abstract algorithmic skeleton another metaheuristic criterion follows a single trajectory that corresponds to a closed walk on a neighbourhood graph, for example, the travelling salesman problem (TSP). The generation of starting points corresponds to jumps in the search space that follow a discontinuous walk to the neighbourhood graph used in the local search. Both trajectory and discontinuous walk use a population of search points or a single search point that is based on a number of iterations of the algorithm. The population is manipulated for a single solution by using Tabu search, simulated annealing, iteration local search and grasp. Moreover, an artificial ant is used to construct solutions guided by the pheromone trails and a heuristic function and genetic algorithms. Using the population-based algorithm provides an easy exploration of the search space.

Ant-Miner was proposed by (Parpinelli et al., 2002). Utilizing ACO techniques, which is a data mining algorithm that is designed to generate classification rules from a given dataset. As for a typical ACO algorithm, the ant is considered an agent that incrementally constructs and modifies a solution from the construction graph to the given problem. The problem is to build a classification model and the solution which is a set of rules that can be used for it. Therefore, each ant in the swarm tries to construct a rule that can be used in the classification model rule set. Basically, Ant-Miner is a rule-based induction algorithm that makes use of ACO's collective behaviour. Ant-Miner deals only with categorical attributes such as continuous (real-valued) attributes discretized as a pre-processing step. Ant-Miner discovers an ordered list of classification rules. For each ant trial, an ant attempts to discover a rule by selecting terms probabilistically according to a heuristic function and pheromone amounts. After a rule is constructed, the ant updates the pheromone on its trail to lead following ants in their paths. The best rule is selected among the ants that have constructed rules and added to the discovered rule set. The algorithm is repeated until the discovered rules cover a sufficient portion of the given dataset. Ant-Miner discovered a rule set that is both simpler and more accurate. Ant-Miner has proved to be a very promising technique for classification rules discovery. Ant-Miner generates a fewer number of rules, lesser number terms per rule, and performs competitively in terms of performance efficiency.

5.2 ANT COLONY OPTIMIZATION

Ant colony optimization (ACO) is one of the swarm intelligent algorithms in nature inspired optimization. The ant moves back and forth in finding the best route in searching for food. A special chemical called pheromone is produced to mark the path during the searching process. The remarkable ant behaviour sparks researchers to further explore the ant's movement in searching for food. Therefore, ACO has been applied in human iris template extraction processes, since a human is also a natural creation suitable for adaptation with natural inspired optimization. In fact, the current technique of searching is limited to finding features such as crypts in human eyes. Moreover, ACO gives a new perspective on the extraction phase, since this approach extracts among the best features of crypts and compares them based on the indexed one in the database. The new approach has been designed towards innovation in reducing error rates in the matching process and thus, providing better detection of iris features in iris recognition. Findings have shown that the matching process in the proposed approach has reduced the Equal Error Rate (EER) to 0.21. Hamming distance rate using the ant indexed features is compared to 0.34 of the HD rate, which is based on non-indexed image matching. However, performance accuracy of the ACO produces on average 76% to 85% accuracy, which does not achieve much improvement compared to previous methods which achieved up to 99.99%.

In Ant Colony Optimization (ACO), the theory of stigmergy was invented by Pierre-Paul Grasse in 1959, which explained the behaviour of building a nest. Dorigo (Dorigo and Gi Di Car, 1994) proposed the ant system and published the ant colony system (ACS) in 1997. ACO is inspired by the capability of artificial ants to perform monitoring and synchronization by searching solutions for local problems. The performance of ACO can be improved by the introduction of an alternative approach called ACS, which focuses mainly on the modification of the transition and pheromone trail update rules, the use of local updates of the pheromone trail to favour exploration, and the use of candidate lists to restrict choices. In fact, it can also be improved by using a crossover mechanism based on the mean of pheromone tables. In iris biometrics, ACO is used in classification and feature selection for extraction.

The strength of the classifier lies in its correct class recognition ability. Various tests have been performed to find the characteristics of the data that determine the performance of classifier. There is no single classifier that works best on all problems. There are a number of classifiers; the most widely used are neural networks, support vector machines, naïve bayes, decision tree classifiers, and many others. Features are the unique information extracted from a given input to be classified by the classifier. These features are used by the classifier to classify the input to a particular class. Features are the result of several operations performed on data as they give specific information about the structure, type, and format of the data.

On the other hand, ACO has been used in face recognition (Grosso et al., 2012). ACO is combined with a modified classifier namely Aggregation Pheromone Density Based Semi-Supervised Classification (APSSC) for automatically updating the changes in biometric templates. The template is representing stored data as ants which is classified into two groups of colonies (client and impostor). The proposed algorithm was produced at cost ratios of 0.1, 1 and 10 with the weighted error rates of 5.55, 5.64, and 2.48. The limitation of this method is that it is slow in processing time and has moderate accuracy since error rate are higher than 4. Another study done by (Kanan et al., 2007) also used ACO as a classifier that was combined with subset feature selection to recognize the human face. The expressions from the human face consist of smiles, anger, happiness and sadness. Simulation results show that the recognition rate is 99.75% and the accuracy is 98.5%. This approach may be suitable for face recognition however but may or not be suitable for iris biometrics. Therefore, an empirical test needs to be conducted for the evaluation of performance accuracy.

For iris biometrics, ACO has been used with neural network classifiers (Ma et al., 2009) and a new scheme is proposed for iris segmentation. The texture segmentation is split into two areas, genuine or not. Until now, finding an effective way for accomplishing these tasks is still a major challenge in practical applications. By defining different kinds of directions on probability and movement difficulty for artificial ants, an ACO based image segmentation algorithm and a texture representation method are then presented for automatic iris image processing. The experimental results indicate that the ACO based image processing methods are competent and quite promising with excellent effectiveness and practicability, especially for images with complex local texture conditions.

However, ACO based image segmentation produces a recognition rate of 93.9% with noise up to 6. Furthermore, as formerly described, image segmentation aims at partitioning an image into several homogeneous disjointed regions. Thus, mechanisms were designed to emphasize the monotony of pixel grey level and local texture similarities. Moving under such supervision, ants tend to roam within homogeneous regions. As a result, the pheromone intensity within each region appeared to be monotone, and left a relatively lower pheromone intensity path between the disjointed regions. Traditionally, an ant tends to maintain its movement direction, and weights for all directions are assigned according to the distortion between the candidate direction and the original direction. That is, if an ant comes from south, and the eight cells have no pheromone, the chance of going north is higher, followed by the chance of going northeast or northwest, and so on, until the likelihood of converging south, becomes very low.

In contrast, a fusion method of ACO, Gabor wavelet and SVM classifier has been introduced by (Kisku et al., 2010) for palm print. The integration of multiple raw palm images at low level has been captured. The captured images later are fused with the palm print instances which is achieved by wavelet transformation and decomposition. In order to capture the palm characteristics, fused image is convolved with the Gabor wavelet transform. The Gabor wavelet feature representation reflects very high dimensional space. Thus, in order to reduce the high dimensionality, the ACO algorithm was applied to select relevant, distinctive, and reduced feature set from the Gabor responses. Finally, the reduced set of features was trained with the support of vector machines and accomplished user recognition tasks. As for evaluation, the CASIA multispectral palm print database was used. The experimental results revealed that the system was found to be robust and encouraging, while variations of classifiers were used. Furthermore, a comparative study of the proposed system is presented with a well-known method.

According to (June et al., 2011), ACO is a better algorithm compared to PSO in terms of accuracy, encoding time performance, and PSNR values. Most of these techniques have and have not been used in iris recognition. The advantages of ACO compared to other bio-inspired algorithms are that it can handle noise better than PSO, gives a good PSNR, performance, and encoding time (June et al., 2011).

Moreover, for a high noise iris environment, ACO is more suitable compared to PSO. This is because ACO tolerates noise since the iris features are constantly changing over time. It is suitable with noisy iris and a template. It is always changing in comparing features and has been proposed using PCA and SVM (Tiwari et al., 2012). Then, ACO is used to replace the PSO since GA+KNN has not been sufficient for feature selection and probabilistic technique for solving computational problems. All these techniques select all iris features from the iris texture regardless of whether they are pigment blotches, crypts, furrows and collarette. A new approach named enhanced ant colony optimization selects the most important unique iris features which naturally adapt to the changes in its characteristics. The unique features are crypts and radial furrows, which both features are stable for a certain time of duration (Shen, 2012) and (Zainal Abidin, 2014). The artificial ant finds the best crypts and radial furrows based on the region of interest using stigmergy analogy, the number of pheromones and the movement of ants forward and backward that finally determine the optimum solution. The optimal solution represents the iris features model for identification and extraction to be used during verification processes.

The comparison is made through the pattern of the iris texture in the confusion matrix and the image-based comparison that is directly made between the iris feature image and the stored one and the performance accuracy is compared with that after the matching process. The motivation that drives the exploration of the ACO is the empirical testing of the theory for detecting the most unique iris features (crypts and radial furrows) for better iris recognition. Figure 17 illustrates the principle of ACO. The basic principle starts when the artificial ants initialize the pheromone values as inputs to construct a probabilistic solution in finding the optimum solution. The construction of solutions is based on colony optimization problems, which emphasis on the basis of components and models. The pheromone values dynamically change the probabilistic solution as the pheromones continuously update the values that the probabilistic solution converges to and called the probabilistic solution map.

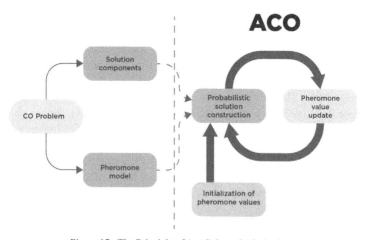

Figure 17: The Principle of Ant Colony Optimization.

Inside the probabilistic solution map contains the strength of the ACO classifier that has an accurate recognition ability class. Various tests have been performed to find the characteristics of the data that determine the performance of the classifier. There is no single classifier that works best on all problems. There are a number of classifiers; the most widely used are neural networks, support vector machines, naïve bayes, decision tree classifiers, and many others. The features are the unique information extracted from a given input to be classified by the classifier. These features are used by the classifier to classify the input to a particular class. The feature is the result of several operations performed on data as it gives specific information about the structure, type, and format of the data.

On the other hand, ACO has been used in face recognition (Kanan et al., 2007) and has been combined with a modified classifier name Aggregation Pheromone Density Based Semi-Supervised Classification (APSSC) for automatically updating the changes in biometric templates. The template represents stored data as ants which is classified into two groups of colonies (genuine and non-genuine). The proposed algorithm produced at cost of ratios of 0.1, 1 and 10 with the weighted error rates were 5.55, 5.64, and 2.48 respectively. The limitation of this method are the slow processing time and moderate accuracy since error rate are higher than 4. Another study done by (Venkatesan, 2010) also used ACO as a classifier that combined subset feature selection to recognize the human face. The features from the human face consist of smiles, anger, happiness and sadness. Simulation results show that the recognition rate is 99.75% and the accuracy is 98.5%. This approach may be suitable for face recognition but may or not be suitable for iris biometrics. Limited study has been done by other researchers on self-learning feature selection using ACO (swarm intelligence algorithm) for iris recognition. Therefore, an empirical test needs to be conducted for the evaluation of performance accuracy.

5.2.1 ACO Algorithm

Ants carry a kind of chemical content, which is called pheromone. The observed intensity of the pheromone influences ants' decision to set a priority in the path selection for the next ant movement. In this way, ants are capable to detect the shortest path from the nest to the food origin. Even if the specifics change, an ant colony can also adapt their scheme to acquire a new shortest path. This content determines the selection they build: the bigger the quantity of pheromone on a path, the higher the chance that an ant choose the path. The quantity of pheromone banked leads other ants going to the path with the firmest density of pheromone.

This cooperative nature of an ant colony enjoys a positive feedback of data. Accommodative interaction of ants leads to emersion of the shortest path. The aspiration of ACO is obtained from such reflections of real ants to resolve discrete optimization problems. The research of ACO on digital images was suggested by (Ramos and Almeida, 2000) and exposed that unreal ant colonies respond and adjust to any type of digital home ground. To section an image, feature differentiation between unlike parts in the image must be established. There are many features of an image, such as object, background, edge, colours, etc. An algorithm was proposed for swarm-based colour segmentation, where two specified types of factors are acquired over RGB images, and result in colour segmentation issues from the swarm behaviour. A study is presented on the edge-detection of different grey-level images with artificial swarm intelligence. It resolves that artificial swarms can do feature extraction in digital images (Salima, 2017). It also presents an evolutionary swarm algorithm for image segmentation where dissimilar populations of individuals compete with each other to invade a bidimensional landscape image to be treated.

The algorithm starts from (i.e., the nest), an ant chooses path e1 or e2 with probability $pi = (1) \tau i \, \tau 1 + \tau 2$, $i = 1, 2$, for reaching the food source vd. If $\tau 1 > \tau 2$, the probability of choosing e1 is higher, and vice versa. For returning from vd to vs, an ant uses the same path as it chose to reach vd, and it changes the artificial pheromone value associated to the used edge.

Having chosen edge ei an ant changes the artificial pheromone value τi as follows: $\tau i \leftarrow \tau i + Q \, li$, where the positive constant Q is a parameter of the model. In other words, the amount of artificial pheromone that is added depends on the length of the chosen path: the shorter the path, the higher the amount of added pheromone.

The foraging of an ant colony in this model is iteratively simulated as follows: At each step (or iteration) all the ants are initially placed in node vs. Then, each ant moves from vs to vd as outlined above. However, in nature, the deposited pheromone is subject to an evaporation over time. Thus, this pheromone evaporation is simulated in the artificial model as follows: $\tau i \leftarrow (1 - \rho) \cdot \tau i$, $i = 1, 2$.

The parameter $\rho \in (0, 1)$ regulates the pheromone evaporation. Finally, all ants conduct their return trip and reinforce their chosen path as outlined above, using the following settings: $l1 = 1$, $l2 = 2$, $Q = 1$. The two pheromone values were initialized to 0.5 each since this would lead to a division by 0. They clearly showed that over time the artificial colony of ants converges to the short path, i.e., after some time all ants use the short path. In the case of 10 ants (i.e., na = 10) the random fluctuations are bigger than in the case of 100 ants. This indicates that the

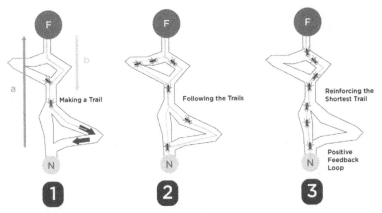

Figure 18: The Shortest Path of Pheromone Trails.

shortest path finding capability of ant colonies results from a cooperation between the ants. Figure 18 illustrates the shortest path finding.

Nevertheless, when optimization problems are considered, pheromone values are associated to solution components instead. Solution components are units from which solutions to the tackled problem are assembled.

In the Travelling Salesman Problem theory (TSP) a completely connected, undirected graph $G = (V, E)$ with edge-weights is given. The nodes V of this graph represent the cities, and the edge weights represent the distances between the cities.

The goal is to find a closed path in G that contains each node exactly once (henceforth called a tour) and whose length is minimal. Thus, the search space S consists of all tours in G. The objective function value $f(s)$ of a tour $s \in S$ is defined as the sum of the edge-weights of the edges that are in s. The TSP can be modelled in many different ways as a discrete optimization problem. The most common model consists of a binary decision variable X_e for each edge in G. If in a solution $X_e = 1$, edge e is part of the tour that is defined by the solution. Concerning the AS approach, the edges of the given TSP graph can be considered solution components, i.e., for each $e_{i,j}$ a pheromone value $\tau_{i,j}$ is introduced . The task of each ant consists in the construction of a feasible TSP solution, i.e., a feasible tour. In other words, the notion of the task of an ant changes from "choosing a path from the nest to the food source" to "constructing a feasible solution to the tackled optimization problem". Note that with this change of task, the notions of nest and food sources lose their meaning. Each ant constructs a solution as follows. First, one of the nodes of the TSP graph is randomly chosen as the starting node. Then, the ant builds a tour in the TSP graph by moving in each construction step from its current node (i.e., the city in which she is located) to another node which she has not visited yet. At each step the traversed edge is added to the solution under construction. When no unvisited nodes are left the ant closes the tour by moving from her current node to the node in which she started the constructing the solution. This way of constructing a solution implies that an ant has a memory T to store the already visited nodes. Each solution construction step is performed as follows. Assuming the ant to be in node v_i, the subsequent construction step is done with probability $p(e_{i,j}) = (4) \tau_{i,j}$! $\{k \in \{1,...,|V|\} | v_k \in /T\} \tau_{i,k}, \forall j \in$ "$1,...,|V| \# , v_j/T$.

Once all ants of the colony have completed the constructing their solution, pheromone evaporation is performed as follows: $\tau_{i,j} \leftarrow (1 - \rho) \cdot \tau_{i,j}, \forall \tau_{i,j} \in T$, (5) where T is the set of all pheromone values. Then the ants perform their return trip. Hereby, an ant—having constructed a solution s—for each $e_{i,j} \in s$ the following pheromone deposit is performed for each: $\tau_{i,j} \leftarrow \tau_{i,j} + Qf(s)$, where Q is again a positive constant and $f(s)$ is the objective function value of the solution s. As explained in the previous section, the system is iterated applying ants per iteration until a stopping condition (e.g., a time limit) is satisfied. Even though the AS algorithm has proved that the ants foraging behaviour can be transferred into an algorithm for discrete optimization, it is generally found to be inferior to the state-of-the-art algorithms. Therefore, over years several extensions and improvements of the original AS algorithm have been explored, which are defined as the ACO metaheuristic.

A. ACO BASED IMAGE SEGMENTATION

Two algorithms are presented at the iris image segmentation and feature texture extraction. The essentials relating to the design of the path probability vector and the movement difficulty are $\Delta((x, y), (x0,y0))$ respectively. Image segmentation aims at moulding an image into various homogeneous disconnected regions. The method is designed to enforce the consistency of pixel grey level and local texture resemblance. Stirring under such the supervision of another ant, the ants move to a series of internal homogeneous regions. Thus, the pheromone intensity inside each region turns out to be monotone, and allows for a relatively lower pheromone intensity paths between disconnect regions.

1) DIRECTION OF LIKELIHOOD VECTOR:

Direction probability vectors are employed to be check in advance and stay unique during the over all ant movement. Traditionally, an ant moves to keep its direction, and weights for all directions are put according to the deformation among the campaigner directions and the original direction, i.e., if an ant arrives from south, and the eight cells have no pheromone, the probability of departing north is higher, adopted by the probability of departing northeast or northwest, and so on, until the likeliness of returning south, which is very low. Here, this mechanism is predetermined, however, 2 standards are applied to imply the landscape information. Thus, the direction likelihood vector defined in

$$P_i^{dir} = P_i^1 + P_i^2 + P_i^3$$

8 neighbouring cells are counted as the 1st cell and the one that arrives in the region is considered counter clockwise, and the others are considered clockwise. The 1st item for each is assigned by the vector, $\left(\dfrac{1}{20}, \dfrac{1}{12}, \dfrac{1}{4}, 1, \dfrac{1}{4}, \dfrac{1}{12}, \dfrac{1}{20} \right)$ which is the basic movement momentum. The 2nd items P_i^2 is arranged according to the resemblance of grey level among the *ith* cell f(i) and the center cell f(0): $P_i^2 = \dfrac{1}{1 + \left| f_{(i)} - f_{(0)} \right|^\beta}$, β

is an experimentally selected parameter to adjust these factors. Clearly, this part reflects the resemblance among neighbouring pixels. The more similar the grey levels of the pixels, the more possible it is that the pixels belong to the same class. The 3rd items are designated by the local texture resemblance among the sub-images W(i) which are covered from the cell, and the centre sub-image W(0): $P_i^3 = \dfrac{1}{1 + \left| d(w_i - w_0) \right|^\gamma} \cdot \gamma$

is also experimentally determined to a certain posing parameter. Here, the centre cell with the 8 neighbours naturally form a 3×3 pixels sub-image W(0). Around W(0), there exit 8 neighbours of 3×3 pixels sub-image too: W(1),W(2),...,W(8), which can be as counted in same path as that for neighbouring cells. The space between 2 sub-images d (W(i), W(0)) represent the histogram length even though it has several classes. The more similar the distributions are, the higher the chance that the sub-images are belonging to the same class.

2) MOVEMENT EFFORT:

Typically, the background object has a darker grey level of an object. The edge points are generally pointing where grey values drastically change. The gradient, which provides a measure of this change, is another important feature to determine edge point from the background or object region. To decrease the pheromone intensity at edge cells, the grey level gradient is simplified as, $\Delta (i,0) = A \cdot P_i^2$ where A is a constant.

- DIRECTION LIKELIHOOD VECTOR:

The generalized form for the direction likelihood vector has the same formula, and the 1st item P_i^3 stays unchanged. However, the 2nd items P_i^3 is now set to emphasize the difference of grey levels between the *ith* cell f(i) and the centre cell f(0): $|f_{(i)} - f_{(0)}|^\beta$. The 3rd items P_i^3 are also given by the local texture difference between the *ith* sub image W(i) and the centre sub image W(0): $|d(w_i - w_0)|^\gamma$

- MOVEMENT EFFORT:

In an attempt to increase the pheromone intensity at edge cells according to texture change, let $\Delta(i,0) = B . P_i^2$, where B is a constant.

5.2.2 ACO Pseudocode

```
The procedure ACO_MetaHeuristic is
    while not_termination do
        generateSolutions()
        daemonActions()
        pheromoneUpdate()
    repeat
end procedure
```

Step-1: Initialize parameters such as α, β, γ, K and A.

```
Initialize pheromone distribution θ(x, y)
```

Step-2: For all ants, arrange: locate each ant agent arbitrarily on the territory array;

Step-3: For t = 1, arrange: Step-4 to Step-12; here controls the maximum iterations.

Step-4: For all ants, arrange: Step-5 to Step-10;

Step-5: Calculate global direction probabilities Pi.

Step-6: Select the adjacent cell with the greatest Pi.

Step-7: If the selected cell is filled by another ant, do: continue for the next ant.

Step-8: Move the ant.

Step-9: Increase the pheromone at the cell.

Step-10: Continue for the next ant.

Step-11: Evaporate pheromone by K, at all cells.

Step-12: Continue for the next iteration.

Step-13: End.

The general procedures on conducting the experiments are as follows:

a) Compare the existing extraction process (texture analysis) with other methods (ACO and PSO) in the same field for obtaining the extraordinary criteria of Enhanced Ant Colony Optimization (EACO),

b) Benchmark the performance accuracy of EACO according to the international biometric standard; and

c) Implement the new approach (EACO) in the extraction process for iris recognition.

Algorithm 1

```
Ant colony optimization (ACO)
while termination conditions not met do
ScheduleActivities
AntBasedSolutionConstruction()
{see Algorithm 2} PheromoneUpdate()
DaemonActions() {optional}
```

Algorithm 2

```
Procedure  AntBasedSolutionConstruction()  of
Algorithm 1 s = '( Determine N (s)
WhileN (s) # = Ø
do c ← ChooseFrom(N (s)) s ← extend s by
appending solution component
Determine N (s)
end while
```

5.2.3 Case Study: Enhanced ACO based Extraction of Iris Template

The Enhanced Ant Colony Optimization approach is a new approach which combines ACO and CBIR techniques. This new approach serves to automatically detect blobs of unique iris features during the extraction process, specifically in high noise iris environments. Traditionally, this process is carried out manually, thus it requires substantial effort, resources and monetary values as well and may be prone to human error. The proposed combination approach aims to alleviate these issues by introducing efficiency in recognition, enhancement in the process of finding optimum solutions and an autonomous detection approach to reduce the EER.

The iris feature has special regions according to the type of blob features for instance crypts, radial furrows and pigment melanin in the ciliary zone. Based on the natural region, the average length of rows for crypts and radial furrows is transformed into mathematical operations to find the approximation of rows for furrows and crypts using the mean formula. The purpose of measuring the length of rows inside the iris feature template is to determine the filter size for crypts and radial furrows.

$$\overline{X} = \frac{\Sigma X}{n}$$

where,

$\overline{X}$ = mean

ΣX = Sum of occurences

n = Total number of occurences

Firstly, iris texture with $[20 \times 240]$ is divided into 3 regions of interest in order for ant1 and ant2 to self-learn in finding the unique iris features (crypts and radial furrows). The region '1' contains the radial furrow, the region '2' consists of crypts and region '3' contains the eyelashes and eyelids. Only region '1' and '2' are selected for iris feature extraction. Secondly, after the weightage is setup as in region '1', the artificial ant starts searching for unique iris features of radial furrows which are at the edge point of the left and upper most part of the matrix (i,j). The ant moves forward starting with 0° and followed with 45°, 90°, 135° and 180° in an anticlockwise manner. Figure 19 illustrates furrow detection with artificial ants' movements.

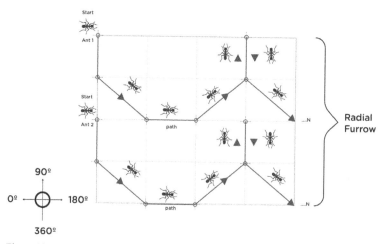

Figure 19: Ant Movements Based on Degrees of Angle (0°, 45°, 90°, 135° and 180°) for Furrow.

Secondly, the ant searches the unique features in the iris template [20 × 240] using angles of degree measures (0°, 45°, 90°, 135° and 180°) and starts from the left upper most point until the end of the matrix in a zig-zag manner. The outcome of this step produces a process called 'weightage' in order to control the ants' movements for searching crypts or furrows in the iris features. For each angle movement starting from 0°, the ant turns to 45°, followed by 90°, 135° and 180°, and the ant moves forward according to path of the movements until the end of the matrix. Each movement on the path is measured in precision (FAR and FRR). As the ant reaches the end of the matrix, it moves backward towards the starting point. This is important in order to complete a loop cycle based on the angle degrees, in which a complete loop represents one time iteration. In order to obtain the complete iris features (radial furrows and crypts), the ant moves forward and backward for 10 iterations in order to obtain convergence.

The mathematical equation for performing iterations for finding radial furrows (at rows 1 to 4) is illustrated in the following Rule.

For k = 0,

$$\vartheta \quad path\_radial\,furrow = \begin{cases} 0^0 & \text{if} & i = 5, 7, 9, 11 & \& \ j = 1 + 3k \\ 45^0 & \text{if} & i = 6, 8, 10, 12 & \& \ j = 1 + 3k \\ 90^0 & \text{if} & i = 6, 8, 10, 12 & \& \ j = 2 + 3k \\ 135^0 & \text{if} & i = 6, 8, 10, 12 & \& \ j = 3 + 3k \\ 180^0 & \text{if} & i = 5, 7, 9, 11 & \& \ j = 1 + 3k \end{cases}$$

where the iteration = k + 1.

On the other hand, for crypt features, the ant movements are illustrated as Figure 20.

For crypt features, the ant movements, as in Equation Pd shows the crypt features at rows numbered 5 to 12. The number of loops for each ant is k+1 and 6 ants are used simultaneously during all 10 iterations. The governing equation of the orientation of ants' movements is in the following Rule.

For k = 0,

$$\vartheta \quad path\_crypt = \begin{cases} 0^0 & if & i = 1, 3 & \& \ j = 1 + 3k \\ 45^0 & if & i = 2, 4 & \& \ j = 1 + 3k \\ 90^0 & if & i = 2, 4 & \& \ j = 2 + 3k \\ 135^0 & if & i = 2, 4 & \& \ j = 3 + 3k \\ 180^0 & if & i = 1, 3 & \& \ j = 3 + 3k \end{cases}$$

where iteration = k + 1.

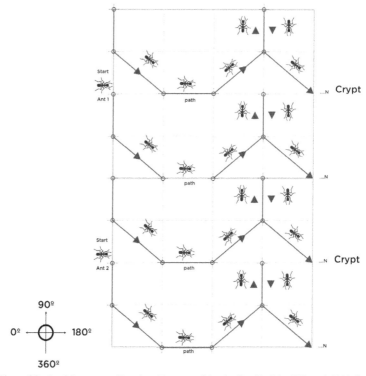

Figure 20: Ant Movements Based on Degrees of Angle (0°, 45°, 90°, 135° and 180°) for Crypt.

For the next iteration, the artificial ant moves from one point to another, t, an ant in point i, chooses the next point j. Based on position of j, the artificial ant moves according to a degree angle where $d \in [1, N]$ (N is the total number of points in the iris search region), each pair wise point (i, j) has (NC − 1)+(NC − 2)+....+2+1 trail values with one for each possible destination point d. An ant located in point i, can have self-determine the final destination. Therefore, the ants adapt their self-searching activity to the varying point characteristics, (Pd).

$$P_d = \sum_{d'=1}^{N} \frac{fjd}{2}$$

The angle in degrees (0°, 45°, 90° and 135°), P_d is a binary label, valued in {0, 1} and the degree vector X = (X(1), . . . , X(q)) models some multivariate observation for predicting P_d, taking its values in a high-dimensional space.

$X \subset Rq, q \geq 1.$

The probability measure on the underlying space is entirely described by the pair (m, n), where m denotes the marginal distribution of X and n(x) is the posterior probability.

$$n(x) = \Sigma_{n\in Nk} \{P_{nd} = 1, \mid X = x\}$$

In maintaining the pheromone trail, τk, the ant relies on a fortification plan. In the context of this study, fortification planning was a back-up plan if the current pheromone update modification did not succeed. The returning mediator updates the pheromone for destination d', and the probability Pfd', according to Equation (4). The factor r is an edge of the region; $r \in (0,1)$ is used by the current point for positive fortification.

$$Pfd' \leftarrow Pfd' + r\ (1 - Pfd')$$

In order to satisfy the constraint, the probabilities of Pnd' for destination d' of the other neighboring points implicitly receive negative fortification by normalization.

$$Pd' \leftarrow Pd' - r\ Pd',\ n \in Nk,\ n \neq f.$$

where the negative fortification.

$$Ps(n,d) \leftarrow Ps(n,d) + \gamma\ Q\text{-}qn/Q$$

$$Q = 1/\mid N\ (s) \mid \Sigma_{k\in N(s)} q_k$$

If $Ps(n,d) < 0$, then substitute 0 for $Ps(n,d)$ or else ∇d, in order to fulfill the requirement,

$$\Sigma_{k\in N(s)}\ Ps(n,d) = 1.$$

Negative fortification is important for erasing the pheromone in local iris maps, which is the unnecessary trail made that has been deleted. In this study, if there are pair wise points blurred or damaged, they helps in determining new pairwise points from one point to the destination point, or else the pheromone update trail ends in the system. When all ants have found a solution, the trails are updated.

$$\tau xy \leftarrow (1 - \rho)\ \tau xy + \Sigma_k \Delta\tau_{xy}^k$$

where,

τxy = the amount of pheromone for state transition xy,

ρ = the pheromone evaporation coefficient

$\Delta\tau_{xy}^k$ = the amount of pheromone for the kth ant, for moves corresponding to the edge of the region map,

$$\Delta\tau_{xy}^k = \begin{cases} I \equiv Q/Lk\ \textit{if ant k uses curve xy in its tour} \\ 0\ \textit{otherwise} \end{cases}$$

where

Lk = cost of the kth ant's tour (typically the distance of end-to-end points)

Q = constant

$\Delta \tau_{xy}^{k}$ determines the values in the region of interest

Qk is equal to I from Equation 3.16. If ant k matches with k-1 iris features at xy, the enhanced ant colony optimization pheromone table is updated, or else vice versa.

Thirdly, the ants' movements are measured with the precision (FAR and FRR) which are based on the enhanced ant colony optimization Pheromone Table. Both ants stop at 10th iterations or converge once. Fourthly, the confusion matrix shows the evaluation function of the feature subsets which are crypt and non-crypt features or radial furrows or non-radial furrows. Lastly, crypt and radial furrow features are indexed using CBIR in order to store into the database for future matching processes.

The crypt and radial furrow shapes are determined through comparison between the values in the updated local ant map and the current position of points in the iris features. Furthermore, the values in the updated ant local map is the crypt or furrow information of a person. Meanwhile, the current position of points indicates the marked shapes of crypts and furrows for a person. The iris features are exclusive which is why one cannot predict the iris feature pattern since the region of interest is based on the iris feature pattern itself. Therefore, precision is used to measure the performance accuracy.

After 10 iterations, the ant movements converge and generate a final construction. The final construction map is saved into a database.

For the matching phase, the iris features images are indexed with an ant feature vector (stored as an index in feature databases) as crypt and furrow indexes. The similarity of the feature index vectors of the query and database images is measured to retrieve the image. Let $\{F(x, y); x = 1, 2, \ldots ,X, y = 1, 2, \ldots ,Y \}$ be a two-dimensional image pixel array. For black and white images, $F(x, y)$ denotes the grayscale intensity value of pixel (x, y). The problem of retrieval is as follows: For a query image Q, we find image T from the image database, such that distance between corresponding feature vectors is less than the specified threshold, i.e., $D(Feature(Q), Feature(T) \leq t$ (1). The co-occurrence matrix $C(i, j)$ counts the co-occurrence of pixels with gray values i and j at a given distance d. The distance d is defined in polar coordinates (d, θ), with discrete length and orientation. In practice, θ takes the values $0°$; $45°$; $90°$; $135°$ and $180°$. G is the number of gray-values in the image, then the dimension of the co-occurrence matrix $C(i, j)$ will be $N \times N$. The co-occurrence matrix $C(i, j)$ is illustrated using pseudocode in Figure 21.

```
Read iris feature template
Define Clique - define angle of degree
Pheromone function initialization
Pheromone setting
Initialization of positions of ants
Save the positions in ant's memory by converting 2D position
into 1D position
Save when ant has reached to the end of memory iterations
Find the neighbourhood of current position
If search clique mode==4 then
 Copy the xxx into the temporary matrix
Else if clique mode==8 then
 Copy the xx features into the temporary matrix
End if
Remove the position of the image range
If neighbour is in the memory then
Recalculate the search
Else
Generate random number to determine next ant position
Save the position of current delta
Update the pheromone function
End of iterations
```

Figure 21: The Pseudocode of Co-occurrence Matrix.

Therefore, the computational complexity of the co-occurrence matrix depends quadratically on the number of gray-scales used for quantization. Moreover, the new ant feature index is compared with the stored image to find the correct match to the genuine which is based on the values of FAR and FRR (dependent variables). The evaluation is tested with other studies for the validation process.

The comparison process redoes the preprocessing and extraction in obtaining the real time iris features. Then, the stored iris features were compared with the real time ones. There are various methods of comparison between the real and stored iris information which can be categorized into two groups (a) block-based matching and (b) pixel-based matching. The block matching compares a string of either one or two dimensional arrays with real and stored iris templates. Meanwhile, the pixel-based matching verifies between stored and real iris features pixel by pixel.

In the block matching, the implementation of the Hamming Distance computation in parallel 32-bit chunks enables extremely rapid comparisons of IrisCodes when searching through a large database to find a match. On a single 300 MHz CPU, such exhaustive searches are performed at a rate of about 100,000 irises per second. On a single 3 GHz server, one million IrisCodes can be compared in about 1 second.

However, when iris features change, the comparison process fails to match due to the flipping bits problem. It is difficult to compare stable iris codes with the unstable iris codes due to the changes in its structure that are affected by aging, distortion and iris deformation. To overcome mis-matching problem, the EACO approach does not compare the iris codes, but evaluates them by using the iris pixel-based matching since pixel values are based on image comparisons.

The main idea is to model the problem to solve the searching problem with a minimum cost path in a region of interest using artificial ants to search for the best paths. The behavior of artificial ants is inspired from real ants: they lay pheromone trails on region components and choose their paths with respect to probabilities that depend on pheromone trails that have been previously laid. However, these pheromone trails progressively decrease by evaporation. Therefore, the proposed comparison used the pixel-based method to measure the shape and pixel values of unique iris features (crypts and radial furrow) in the iris texture.

In finding the similarity model of iris features in the iris feature database, the clustering method used in ACO is to determine the iris features dataset at random. At each forward and backward cycle, each ant constructed a complete matching in a randomized way, and then, the pheromone trails were updated. Intuitively, this indirect stigmergic communication aimed at giving information about the quality of path components in order to attract ants, in the following iterations, towards the corresponding areas of the search space. The clustering from trees element used limited parameters to discriminate them faster into classes. The enhanced ant colony optimization searched the similarity in the trees that followed the classical Ant Colony Optimization algorithmic scheme for static combinatorial optimization problems. The algorithm stopped iterating, either when an ant had found an optimal matching, or when a maximum number of cycles had been performed. On the other hand, if there was no match for 'similarity' in iris features, the crypts and radial furrow were labeled as non-genuine and non-crypt and non-furrow too in the database.

The matching process is carried out using Hamming distance as a metric for iris recognition and gives a measure of how many bits are the same between two bit patterns. In comparing the bit patterns T and P, the Hamming Distance (HD) is defined as the sum of disagreeing bits (sum of the exclusive-OR between T and P) over N, the total number of bits in the bit pattern.

$$HD = \frac{1}{N} \Sigma_i^N \oplus \quad Pi$$

where,

N = total number of bits

T_i = Stored iris templates

P_i = Real iris templates

The matching process starts by reading the iris template from left to right to the end of the arrays using a zig zag manner in the respective regions. Ants search for the best matched point with strong subsets of the iris features in the matching phases which consist of verification and identification. For the verification mode, each crypt and furrow index values are compared pixel by pixel to find the similarity between two iris templates. Conversely, in identification mode, the proposed approach uses the Hamming distance to measure the nearest neighbor based on the point.

Performance had been evaluated using two performance measures: precision and recognition rate. The formula for recognition rate is 100% indicating a percentage of the error rate. On the other hand, the precision is the ratio of the number of correct retrieved images to the total number of images in the retrieved dataset. The optimization time is important to measure the different time allocation for searching the unique iris features in both the existing and the new model. To setup the experimental test bed using the swarm approach requires specific settings and adjustment as described in Sections 5.2.3.1 and 5.2.3.2.

5.2.3.1 Experiment Environment Ant Colony Optimization (ACO)

In order to utilize ACO in this work, the experiments conducted are based on parameters leading to a better convergence which are tested. The best parameters that are obtained by simulations are as follows: $\alpha = 1$, $\beta = 2$, evaporation rate $\rho = 0.95$, the initial pheromone intensity of each arc (seed) is equal to 1, the number of ants in each iteration $m = 2, 4, 6, 8$ and 10, and the maximum iterations $k = 50$. To evaluate the average classification accuracy of the selected feature subsets, 10-fold cross validation (CV) is used.

The experimental setup in this work utilizes MATLAB® R2010 software packages to program the image formulation of crypts and radial furrows using Enhanced Ant Colony Optimization algorithms. Once the image of iris features (crypt and radial furrows) is obtained, Content Based Information Retrieval (CBIR) is used to index iris features (crypt and radial furrows) before it is saved into the database.

Lastly, both ants stop at 10th iterations or converge once. However, according to previous works, the identification of stable iris features is still conducted using manual observation and image editing. This means that a person has to manually crop or locate the shapes of crypts and radial furrows before further processing.

Thus, the detection of micro characteristics in iris feature is based on Pi and Ti.

$$P_t = T_t . \Delta T_t$$

Where

$$T_t = (1 - \rho) . \alpha + (\rho \frac{1}{buffer})^\beta$$

Subsequently, the following experimental parameters have been configured:

$\alpha = 1$;

$\beta = 2$,

$\rho = 0.95$

$\pi = 0.05$;

ant memory buffer $= 40$

clique mode is 4 or 8.

The initial pheromone intensity of each arc is equal to 1, the number of ants in each iteration $m = 10$ and the maximum iterations $k = 50$. Each ant's movements (forward and backward) consist of the number of iterations which are measured based on the precision and recall parameters. Precision is defined as a repetitive measurement of the number of ant iterations to find the similar points of crypts and furrows. There are 3 precision measurement parameters used in this work: (i) FAR, (ii) FRR and (iii) ERR values. If they all have the same values, then it indicates that the algorithm provides a high precision output. In contrast, if the FAR, FRR and ERR values are not the same, it indicates a low precision output, thus it also shows that there is variation in the ant's movement.

Once the optimum output is obtained, the visual images of crypts and collarette are indexed in the database using query-image-id and image-tag commands in the CBIR. The indexed image template is then tagged with an ant pheromone field table. At the same time, the stigmergy table is renewed in keeping the latest information from ants and CBIR. After being tagged and indexed, all the visual images are stored into the database for the matching process.

The experiment is designed according to the planning in precision measurement in order to accomplish accuracy. The first column shows the percentage of training that represents the area of space (city) covered by ants to search stable features. The second column shows the number of iterations for ants to move forward and backward in finding the optimal solution to obtain the best pixels points. The third and fourth column is used to measure the FAR and FRR obtained from each iteration. Next, the fifth and sixth column isused to measure the precision and recall values.

5.2.4 The Experiment Results and Findings

The first phase starts with loading the eye image of a person selected from the iris database. The second phase involves the segmentation and normalization phase that is represented in 'Process' buttons using Hough Transform algorithms. Figure 22 presents the third phase that extracts the blob of iris features using Enhanced Ant Colony Optimization that is shown in button 'ANT'. After clicking the 'ANT' button, the blob of iris features (crypts and furrows) has been obtained. Then, the crypts and furrows have been detected, and the proposed approach, searches for the best crypt and furrow shapes. After the best crypts and furrows were obtained, Enhanced Ant Colony Optimization marked their locations in the region. This experiment stores the marked features into the indexed features format. The crypt and furrow indexed features are compared with the ones in the last phase, called matching.

The results from the developed prototype have been able to detect the genuine users accurately compared to the current system. It is apparent from these systems that the features with lower EER can be

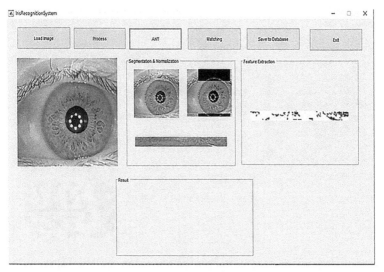

Figure 22: Enhanced Ant Colony Optimization Extraction Interface.

recognized and compared to the existing system. The outcome of the experiment states that the real user can be classified as genuine, as shown in Figure 23. Moreover, if another eye image is loaded in the developed system, then Enhanced Ant Colony Optimization states that the user is not genuine when the Hamming Distance is more than 0.25 HD, in Figure 24.

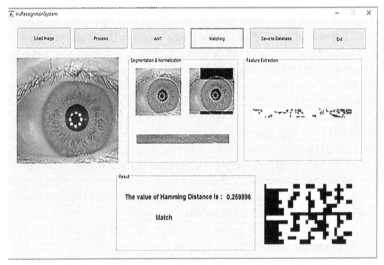

Figure 23: Enhanced Ant Colony Optimization Matching Interface—Match.

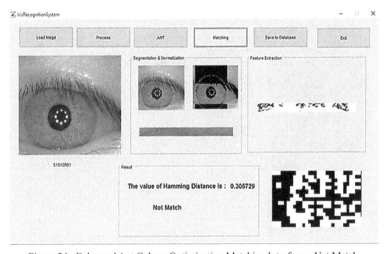

Figure 24: Enhanced Ant Colony Optimization Matching Interface—Not Match.

In Enhanced Ant Colony Optimization, the iris texture is read from the upper left most to the entire array to find the contrast in pixel values. At first, to find the iris features, the iris template is divided into three parts. Then, the artificial ants search for features that are based on degree angles from 0°, 45°, 90°, 135° and 180°. In fact, the ant movements are based on the number of iterations to obtain the best points inside the iris features (crypt and radial furrows).

A reliable solution on unique iris blob features with the indexing process have been obtained through the use of Enhanced Ant Colony Optimization. Interestingly, the blob of iris features image (crypt and radial furrows) shapes is marked as a sequence of unique shapes inside the iris features. Moreover, the marked blob shapes of iris features are indexed based on the best crypts or furrows since there is an observation that a crypt consists of various smaller crypts inside the shape. In fact, the radial furrow is detected to be obviously seen although in a very highly distorted iris image. The indexed crypts and furrows are then put into a two-dimensional array as a string of information of the genuine user before being stored into a database. The stored iris is compared with the real iris image in the comparison phase as illustrated in Figure 25. If the value of Hamming Distance is within the threshold then the iris template is a match and if the value is more, then the iris template is a mismatch.

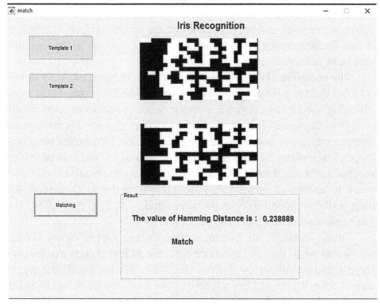

Figure 25: Indexed Iris Feature Retrieval Database.

In this stage, the experiment is conducted on the feature selection implementation based on ACO. The development of the proposed method uses a MATLAB environment for data analysis. This input dataset consists of 5 iris images samples from each of 120 different individuals. In addition, these samples have different characteristics of iris data, such as light intensity, clear or blurry image and noises.

Experiments conducted (Shen, 2012) have classified that the noisy iris contains a valuable noise that can be accepted for further processing in the comparison phase. In fact, the increasing number of noises in the iris affect the accuracy and performance in iris recognition.

Furthermore, researches have been done to overcome the increment of error rates, nevertheless, the reality of the problem is a noisy iris. To date, the iris recognition is at the cutting edge in providing a higher accuracy for faster performance to users. The crypt and radial furrow shapes of stable iris features have been identified through literature review.

The ACO has been compared with PSO since both techniques have been used for iris recognition in biometrics. The experiment also indicates that ACO is better in terms of accuracy, compared to PSO. In order to measure accuracy, the proposed approach is to analyse the relationship between precision versus the recall value. Precision means number of successful detections of unique shapes inside the iris features. Recall means when the precision is average, the pre-selection in image-based iris extraction is determined. Generally, a linear relationship between precision and recall means that the image retrieval is efficient. A non-linear relationship indicates that the accuracy in iris recognition cannot be achieved.

The precision values obtained for CASIA.v3 based on ACO is 0.69 which indicates a linear graph. However, the precision was 0.004 using PSO displayed a vertical graph, which indicated a not linear relationship.

The outcome of this experiment designates that PSO is not a noise tolerant technique and it is not suitable for iris biometrics templates since iris templates have a high noise rate. Thus, PSO does not give high precision compared to ACO. Based on precision and recall experiments result in an overall performance accuracy. With the ACO method, the noise value is around 0.05 on the other hand, with PSO it is 0.068. The PSO error rate is found to be higher than in ACO.

Strong evidence of Enhanced Ant Colony Optimization criteria was found when the new approach was able to find unique iris features (crypts and radial furrows) from the noisy iris image. There was a significant achievement in performance accuracy results shown in radial furrows which are detectable by Enhanced Ant Colony Optimization, despite a noisy iris image environment. Conversely, in a high quality iris feature image, the radial furrow is detected with high precision but moderate performance accuracy. Meanwhile, crypts have shown higher performance accuracy compared to radial furrow feature detection.

5.3 PARTICLE SWARM OPTIMIZATION

In swarm intelligence, the particle swarm optimization (PSO) technique is inspired by the behaviour of social organisms in groups such as the motion of a flock of birds or groups of fish moving from one place to another to find food and the best place to breed. The art of movements have several patterns indicating a method of communication within the group in finding the best location of land based coordinate points. Naturally, the leader sends instructions to the swarm for directions to land safely.

In 1995, Kennedy and Eberhart used PSO in solving complex mathematical problems. The winning points of PSO in handling complex problems are due to its metaheuristic algorithm capability. It acts as a randomly generated population and utilizes a fitness value to evaluate the population. In fact, PSO updates the population and searches for the optimum value with random techniques. Classically, in the population, the new location of each particle is determined by a velocity term, which reflects the attraction of the global best and its own best during the history of the particle and random coefficients, for the following iterations.

Moreover, it has more effective memory capability since each of the particles remembers its own previous neighbourhood best value, which is easier to be implemented having fewer parameters to adjust. In PSO, only the 'best' particle shares the information with others in a one-way information sharing mechanism; the evolution is determined to provide for the best solution. As known, there is no parameter controlling the progression of best neighbourhood values in the general flow of PSO. However, the need of PSO parameters is vital for determining the optimal network structure and hyper parameter configuration for insufficient particles which are unable to improve their best individual positions value before finalising the model.

The selection of PSO parameters can have a huge impact on the optimisation performance. Selecting PSO parameters that yield good performances has therefore been the subject of much research. In this research, the parameters for PSO are determined from the literature review, and trial and error experiments. The parameters that need to be tuned in are as follows:

i. Initialization: A starting point in a random population for initialization of parameters and parameter values in functions. Initialization of the particles is vital in PSO performance because fit is not good then the algorithm may search in irrelevant areas and making it difficult to find the optimal solution. The performance of PSO depends on the initialization of swarms and the different variants of PSOs with respect to initialization.

ii. Population size: The swarm size affects the PSO performance. Very few particles prompt the algorithm to get trapped in local optima. Meanwhile too many particles slow down performance.

iii. Dimension of particle: It is determined by the problem to be optimised.

iv. Maximum velocity: This parameter determines how large should each step taken by each particle should be through the solution space. If it is too big, the particles move erratically and are swiftly attracted to the global best (gbest) without enough exploration of the search space. Hence, they may exceed the search space and the risk of getting trapped in false optima will then increase.

v. Inertia weight (w): Inertia weight provides a balance between the exploration and exploitation processes. Thus, it is considered to be critical for the PSO's convergence behaviour.

vi. Acceleration constant (c1, c2): This parameter is not too critical for PSO's convergence but, proper fine-tuning may result in a faster convergence and alleviation of local minima.

vii. Random number (rand1, rand2): Random numbers are used to maintain the diversity of the population and they are uniformly distributed in the range [0, 1].

viii. The stopping condition: The maximum number of iterations and minimum error requirement are the termination criterion conditions. This condition depends on the problem to be optimised.

The parameter setting of PSOs is based on Epochs, Error goal, population size, acceleration constant (c1,c2), inertia weight (w) and maximum velocity. The Epochs is set to 150. Error goal is 0.01 in population size of 10. The acceleration constants c1 and c2 are initiated at 0.8. Inertia weight is 1.2 and maximum velocity is 0.5.

The performance of each particle is measured using a fitness function which depends on the optimisation problem (Bai, 2010). Each particle i flies through the n-dimensional search space Rn and maintains the following information:

- Xi, the current position of the particle i(x-vector)
- Pi, the personal best position of the particle i(p-vector)
- Vi, the current velocity of the particle i(v-vector).

The personal best position associated with a particle i is the best position that the particle has visited so far. If f denotes the fitness function, then, the personal best of particle i at a time step t is updated as:

$Pi(t+1)=\{(Pi(t)$ if $f(xi(t+1))\geq f(Pi(t))@ x\_i(t+1)$ if $f(xi(t+1))<f(Pi(t)))$

The velocity updates are calculated as a linear combination of position and velocity vectors. Thus, the velocity of a particle I is updated as:

$v\_i(t+1)=wv\_i(t)+c\_(1)r\_(1)(p\_(1)(t)-x\_i(t)+c\_2r\_(2)$ crypt$-x\_i(t))$

while the position of particle i is updated as:

$x\_i(t+1)=x\_i(t)+v\_i(t+1)$

where,

v_i must be in a predefined range [V_min, V_max], where

if $v\_i>V\_max$ then $v\_i=V\_max$, and if $v\_i<V\_min$ then $v\_i=V\_max$.

In the formula, w is the inertia weight, c_1 and c_2 are the acceleration constants, and r_1 and r_2 are random numbers in the range [0, 1]. Moreover, pi is the position of the particle i and the crypt is the updated crypt.

An illustration on how the velocity moves and updates is shown in the Figure 26. Any particle moves in the direction of its best position to its best global position in the course of each generation. The initial position and velocity of a particle are generated randomly. Let the position and velocity of the ith particle in the n-dimensional search space be represented as Pi=[pi,1,pi,2,...,pi,n] and Vi=[vi,1,vi,2,...,vi,n], respectively. Meanwhile, according to a specific fitness function, let the local best of the ith particle be denoted as Pil =[pli,1,pli,2,...,pli,n] and

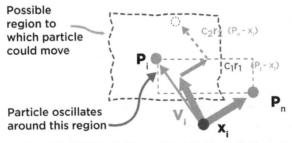

Figure 26: A 2D Velocity Movement and Updates on Regions.

the global best found so far be denoted as Psl =[psl1,psl2,…,psln]. When the crypt image has been identified by the PSO, the label matrix converts the iris template into RGB images to find the edge of crypt.

5.3.1 PSO Algorithm

The implementation of searching for a crypt using the PSO approach has been categorised into three modules. All modules are arranged according to the PSO process. In this research, MATLAB has been used as the main platform in developing the proposed method. The complete operation of particle swarm optimisation is specified below:

Module 1: Initialisation

PSO is initialized with a group of random particles (solutions) and then searches for optima by updating generations. In the beginning, a number of particles, minimum and maximum boundary search space, velocity and position need to be initialised. The preliminarily search of a suitable number of particles is four and the number of iterations is set to 100 due to faster convergence, while the initial velocity and position is set to 0. Each particle represents the pixel values in the iris template.

Algorithm 1

Do
% Initialise number of particles
% Initialise maximum and minimum boundary search space
% Initialise velocity and position
N = 150; %predefined PSO population for multi-segmentation
level = 2;
  N_PAR = level-1; %number of thresholds (number of levels-1)
  N_GER = 150; %number of iterations of the PSO algorithm
  PHI1 = 0.8; %individual weight of particles
  PHI2 = 0.8; %social weight of particles
  W = 1.2; %inertial factor
  vmin=-5;
  vmax=5;
For each particle
Particles are randomly positioned in search space
End
End

Module 2: Calculate Fitness, pBest, gBest and Velocity

All particles have fitness values which are evaluated by the fitness function to be optimized, and have velocities which direct the if flying.

The particles fly through the problem space by following the current optimum particles. PSO is initialized with a group of random particles (solutions) by b searches for optima by updating generations. In every iteration, each particle is updated by following two "best" values. The first one is the best solution (fitness) it has achieved so far. (The fitness value is also stored.) This value is called $p$best. Another "best" value that is tracked by the particle swarm optimizer is the best value, obtained so far by any particle in the population. This best value is a global best and called $g$best. When a particle takes part of the population as its topological neighbours, the best value is a local best and is called $l$best.

Algorithm 2

Do
For each particle
If the fitness value is better than the best fitness value (pBest) in history
        set current value as the new pBestEnd
End
Choose the particles with the best fitness value of all particles as the gBest
For each particle
        % Calculate the particle velocity and update the particle positioning
if size(I,3)==1 %grayscale image
        [aR,bR] = max (fitR);
                if (fitR(bR) > gbestvalueR)
gBestR=xR(bR,:)-1;
gbestvalueR = fitR(bR);
End
End

Module 3: Stop Checking

The algorithm repeats the Modules 2 until certain terminating conditions are met. The termination conditions are met when gBest achieves the objective function where the best crypt is found.

Algorithm 3

Do
If global best achieves the objective function
Terminate the iteration
End
End

The performance of the PSO is much better if it is enhanced or combined with another method in order to achieve a lower EER in the iris recognition system. Due to this demand, a combination model of iris recognition using particle swarm optimization and three other methods like nearest neighbour, bilinear and Bi-Cubic interpolation are under study. These three techniques are a technique that interpolates a 2D image into a new image size and the output image quality is improved. According to the PSNR values, a combination of three techniques shows that Bi-Cubic interpolation is gives better values of PSNR (Nurul et al., 2016) since the crypt image is enlarged for better view. The particles in PSO searches the most optimal crypt features in iris texture meanwhile, the bi-cubic interpolation technique creates sharp and refined crypt images to be indexed and stored into the iris features database and made available for future matching processes.

Bi-Cubic Interpolation is a technique for sharpening and enlarging crypt images and commonly used in computer image editing software for upscaling or resampling the crypt image. In general, Bi-cubic Interpolation are of two types adaptive and non-adaptive. In this case, the non-adaptive algorithm is implemented for detecting the crypt image using the nearest neighbour, bilinear, bicubic and spline. Moreover, bi-cubic interpolation allows for smoother resampling with little image artefacts and giving the best image quality.

The performance of each particle is measured using a fitness function which depends on the optimization problem (Bai, 2010), (Baker, 2006). Each particle i flies through the n-dimensional search space R^n and maintains the following information:

- X_i, the current position of the particle i(x-vector)
- P_i, The personal best position of the particle i(p-vector)
- V_i, the current velocity of the particle i(v-vector).

The personal best position associated with a particle i is the best that the particle has visited so far. If f denotes the fitness function, then the personal best of particle i at a time step t is updated as:

$$Pi(t+1) = \begin{cases} Pi(t) & \text{if } f(xi(t+1)) \geq f(pi(t)) \\ x_i(t+1) & \text{if } f(xi(t+1)) < f(pi(t)) \end{cases} \tag{1}$$

In order to locate the position yielding the lowest error among all the Pi is called the global best position and is denoted as gbest:

$$gbest \in \{P0(t), P1(t), \ldots, Pm(t)\} = \min\{f(P0(t)), f(P1(t)), \ldots, f(Pm(t))\}$$

The velocity updates are calculated as a linear combination of position and velocity vectors. Thus, the velocity of a particle I is updated using $x_i(t+1) = x_i(t) + v_i(t+1)$ and the position of particle I is updated using:

$$v_i(t+1) = wv_i(t) + c_1 r_1 (p_1(t) - x_i(t)) + c_2 r_2 \, crypt - x_i(t))$$

where,

v_i must be in a predefined range $[V_{min}, V_{max}]$, where

if $v_i > V_{max}$ then $v_i = V_{max}$, and if $v_i < V_{min}$ then $v_i = V_{max}$.

In the formula, w is the inertia weight, c_1 and c_2 are the acceleration constants and r_1 and r_2 are random numbers in the range [0, 1]. Moreover, pi is the personal position of the particle i and crypt is the updated crypt.

To employ PSO in the feature selection process, several important parameters, namely alpha (α), beta (β) and sigma (σ), need to be set up for the training process, which depend on the independent validation set and fitness value for each individual. The setting for sample training is defined based on samples and the rest of the remaining data is used for testing. To find the optimal solution, the best configuration of parameter settings across a range of values must be determined.

Furthermore, the data set is split into 10 subsets of equal size and this process is executed 10 times. In order to obtain the accuracy rate of the classification for each selected feature subset, 9 of the 10 subsets were used as training data while the remaining single subset was used for testing the data. This cycle is then repeated with the second sub-sample (10 subsets) for the rest of the overall data set.

For comparison purposes, the number of particles (population size) was set to 5, 20 and 100 and fitness function, σ, was set at 0.95. Meanwhile, α was set for 10 folds of cross validation for training and testing with respect to different parameter values of alpha(α)=1 and beta(β)=2.

Bi-cubic interpolation interpolates a 2D image into a new sized crypt image. In this method, the nearest 16 pixels are used to create an intermediate pixel F(p'q'). Therefore, the output image quality is improved. An intermediate pixel F(p'q') that is Near to F(p,q) is created by interpolating nearest [4 x 4] pixels from F(p–1,q–1) to F(p+2,q+2), then interpolating the results in the horizontal direction. A 2D illustration on how Bi-Cubic Interpolation moves is shown in Figure 27.

The following equation (Gao, 2011) is used to interpolate nearest 16 pixels. Number 2 on the sigma represent number of loops in the shaded code.

$$F(p',q') = \sum_{m=-1}^{2} \sum_{n=-1}^{2} F(p+m,q+n) R_C \{(m-a)\} R_C \{-(n-b)\}$$

Where F(p + m, q + n) indicates pixel's data at location (p + m, q + n). Rc() denotes a Bi-Cubic interpolation function such as a BSpline, Traingular and Bell cubic.

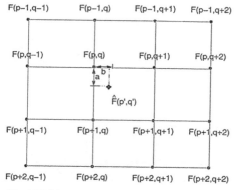

Figure 27: A 2D Movement of Bi-Cubic Interpolation (Gao, 2011).

5.3.2 Case Study: The Proposed Design and Approach Method

The PSOBCI method consists of three main phases, which is pre-processing, feature extraction, comparison, and, testing and validation. The pre-processing phase involves few steps of process implementation that is image acquisition, segmentation and normalization.

5.3.2.1 Experimental Environment for Particle Swarm Optimization (PSO)

The implementation of PSO and BCI algorithms for the suggested iris recognition system was implemented using MATLAB 2012. Experiments were conducted is based on the selected 100 images of 10 persons (each with 10 images). The number of particles (population size) was set to 5, 20 and 100 and fitness function, σ, was set at 0.95. Meanwhile, α was set for 10 folds of cross validation for training and testing with respect to different parameter values of alpha(α)=1 and beta(β)=2. Furthermore, the data set was split into 10 subsets with equal size and this process was executed 10 times. In order to obtain the accuracy rate of the classification to each selected feature subset, 9 of the 10 subsets were used as training data while the remaining 1 subset was used as testing data. This cycle is then repeated with the second sub-sample (10 subsets) for the rest of the overall data set.

5.3.2.2 Pre-Processing Phase

Image acquisition is a process of acquiring a photo from a human iris. This stage is one of the important processes since the success of the recognition stages is dependent on the quality of the images taken from the iris during image acquisition stage. Additionally, if visible light is used during imaging for those individuals whose iris is dark, a slight contrast comes to exist between the iris and the pupil, which makes it difficult to differentiate between the two areas of the feature.

The next process is the segmentation that assists to localize the two iris boundaries namely, inner boundary of iris-pupil and the outer one of the iris-sclera and to localize eyelids. In segmentation stage, it includes the three following steps.

Iris inner boundary localization with regard to illumination intensity is very different in inner and outer pupillary parts, and the pupil is darker compared to the iris. The use of Canny edge detection in the pre-processing stage results in determining points in the iris pupil boundary. As it could be observed, pupillary boundary is almost completely detected. After determining edge points, by the use of circular Hough Transform, the center and radius of iris circle are obtained.

After that, iris outer boundary localization is applied. This process is the most important and challenging stage of segmentation in detecting the boundaries of the iris and the sclera. Firstly, because there is usually no specific boundary in this area and illumination intensity distinction between iris and sclera is very low at the border. Secondly, there are other edge points in the eye image in which illumination intensity distinction is much more than that of the boundary of the iris and sclera. As a result, edge detection algorithms which are able to detect outer iris edges identify those points as the edge. Therefore, in order to detect the outer boundary of the iris, these points have to be identified and eliminated.

In the CASIA Iris Image-Interval database, the localization of the boundary between the eyelids and the iris is applied to find the boundary as two lines as the first order estimate. To localize them, after detecting edges and by the use of linear Hough transform, the properties of the lines could be obtained. The initial eyelids boundary is detected using canny edge detection to identify few localized boundaries through this method for some eye images. This method could result in a false outcome only for some images which have too many patterns in the iris tissue when the edges of these patterns are detected by canny edge detection.

In the normalization stage, an approach based on Daugman's method is used that transforms the iris area from polar to Cartesian coordinates. Therefore, the iris area is obtained as a normalized strip with regard to the iris boundaries and the pupillary center. In order to transform the iris area from polar to Cartesian coordinates, 128 pupils-centered perfect circles are chosen starting from the iris-pupil boundary and then the pixels located on these circles are mapped into a rectangle.

As a result, the iris area which looks like a circular strip is converted into a rectangular strip. Since with changes in the surrounding illumination level, the size of the pupil is adjusted by the iris to control the amount of light entering the eyes. It is also possible that an individual's distance with a camera could be different, and the iris is not the same size in different images. Therefore, choosing these 128 perfect circles normalizes the iris in terms of size as well. Then, the illumination intensity in segmented iris tissue is tuned to obtain for image contrast to bring more clarity into the iris tissue. In the initial stage, localization of circular iris inner and outer boundaries, of eyelids is implemented; later 128 circles in the iris area are chosen, and eventually transformed from polar to Cartesian coordinates. The next phase is feature extraction.

5.3.2.3 Feature Extraction Phase

After the pre-processing phase is done with segmentation and normalization, the second phase is feature extraction. In order to extract the discriminating features from the normalized, PSO and Bi-Cubic Interpolation the patterns are normalized.

Three processes split the iris template into 4 blocks, by applying PSO to search the best point of the crypt feature and Bi-Cubic Interpolation finds the region of crypts.

The first process splits the iris template in to 4 blocks using split block in MATLAB software. (Miyazawa, 2008) used split block in the matching phase to reduce the size of iris image. Besides that (Guang Zhu, 2006) used sub blocks to identify eyelids and eyelashes in the iris template. Due to their study splitting the image into blocks has gave the system a more accurate performance. Therefore, split block have been used in this study to separate the image from the important parts of the iris template. The iris template is split into 4 blocks and only the upper left block is used to identify the crypt using PSO. The best crypt is saved in the database for the first-time enrolment, while for the second time enrolment it performs a comparison with the existing crypts in the database.

The second process is PSO. In this process, PSO works as a group and each particle keeps track of its own position and velocity in the problem space. Any particle can move in the direction of its personal best position to its best global position in the course of each generation. The initial position and velocity of a particle are generated randomly. Let the position and velocity of the ith particle in the n-dimensional search space be represented as $Pi=[pi,1,pi,2,...,pi,n]$ and $Vi=[vi,1,vi,2,...,vi,n]$, respectively. Meanwhile, according to a specific fitness function, let the local best of the ith particle be denoted as $Pil=[pli,1,pli,2,...,pli,n]$ and the global best found so far be denoted as $Psl=[psl1,psl2,...,psln]$. When the crypt image has been identified, the label matrix converts the iris template into an RGB image to find the edge of the crypt. Then, the Bi-Cubic interpolation process is applied to find the region of interest that consists of crypts by enlarging the images of the crypts. After that, the images of the crypts are saved in the database.

5.3.2.4 Comparison Phase

The comparison phase involves two process, which are verification or matching and identification. In this phase the stored iris features are compared with the real ones. The identification mode compares the real iris code with the representative model of multiple iris images in finding the similarities using one-to-many techniques. Meanwhile, the verification mode finds the similarities in one-to-one iris features images. However, the new model needs to compare between the iris features values. The value may not be the same but as long as it is within the range of values meaning that the matching is 'true' else it falls under a different range that represent the furrows. As long as they are in the range, the pixel values are compared to the real and stored iris features.

5.3.2.5 Testing and Validation Phase

The evaluation process in iris recognition is done at this phase where the performance of iris recognition is evaluated by using False Rejection Rate (FRR) and False Acceptance Rate (FAR).

The achievement of iris authentication is calculated with Equal Error Rate (EER). However, the performance of the PSO is much better if it is combined with other methods. Therefore, the purpose of this study is to fulfill the demand of achieving high accuracy and reducing the percentage of non-genuine user increments. Due to this demand, a new model of iris recognition using combination of particle swarm optimization and Bi-cubic interpolation is presented in selecting the best iris feature (crypt) among unique iris features. The reasons for proposing PSOBCI are due to the strengths from PSO and the interpolation.

Bi-cubic interpolation is a technique that interpolates a 2D image into new crypt image size. In this method, the nearest 16 pixels are used to create an intermediate pixel $F(p'q')$. Therefore, the output image quality is improved. In the Figure below, an intermediate pixel $F(p'q')$ [Near to $F(p,q)$] is created by interpolating nearest [4 x 4] pixels from $F(p-1,q-1)$ to $F(p+2,q+2)$, then interpolating the results in the horizontal direction.

In order to find the shape of the crypt in the iris template Bi-Cubic Interpolation is applied. There are four main modules in this technique. The first step is initializing the iris template image. After applying Bi-Cubic interpolation the iris template image is saved in the database, which is stored in the MySQL database. During the connection to MySQL, another linker tool is used known as XAMPP. In this case,

XAMPP needs to be activated before turning on the connection between MATLAB and MySQL.

Module 1: Intake

Do

   Read iris image

End

Module 2: Read Coordinates

   The second module is identifying the current location or coordinate of the iris in the iris template. Then, Bi-Cubic interpolation is used to find the region of the crypts.

Do

   Read the coordinates and find the region of crypts

End

Module 3: Creates New Coordinates

   The third module creates the new coordinates of the crypts. In this module the image of the crypt is created by interpolating nearest 4 x 4 pixels from $F(p-1, q-1)$ to $F(p=2,q+2)$, then interpolating the results in the horizontal direction.

Do

   For i=1:256, for j=1:256;
     x1(i,j)=a*x(i,j);
     y1(i,j)=y(i,j)/a;

End

End

Module 4 : Interpolation

Start

   Perform interpolation

End

5.3.3 Identification Phase in Iris Recognition System

Identification phase is carried out by capturing one or more eye image data and comparing the iris pattern with images stored in the database. The details of process in identification are discussed in 5.3.3.1 until 5.3.3.2.

5.3.3.1 Image Acquisition

Image acquisition is the first part in the identification phase. In this experiment, CASIA database of the human eye image has been used which is CASIA-Iris-Interval subset of the CASIA v3.0 database. The size of the iris images is in [320x280 pixels] from 249 subjects. The process of acquisition in the enrolment part is using the image processing but each eye of 249 subjects is captured 5 times in the interval time. The purpose of acquiring iris images 5 times per image in the enrolment part is to assist the classifier to ascertain the changes in the iris image of the same subject and it would be useful in the matching process.

5.3.3.2 Segmentation and Normalization

The second phase in identification is segmentation and normalization of the image. In this phase the iris image is localized to detect the outer and inner boundaries and transform them into unwrapped counter-clockwise to fixed size rectangular texture by using Hough transform technique. The size of the template after the normalization is done is 240 x 20. Segmentation and normalization processsare shown in the Figure 28.

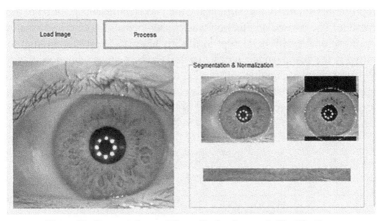

Figure 28: Segmentation and Normalization Process in Identification.

5.3.3.3 Particle Swarm Optimization (PSO) and Bi-Cubic Interpolation (BCI) Process

After the iris image is transformed into the template image, it is the ability of extracting some unique attributes from iris, which helps to generate a specific code for each individual in the next step. PSO and Bi-Cubic Interpolation are typically used for analyzing the human iris patterns and extracting features from them to find the best crypt, for the feature Extraction steps. The initial steps split the iris template image, then apply PSO to find the best crypt and the final step is Bi-Cubic Interpolation.

• **Split Iris template image**

The Iris image template needs to be split in the first process. In this step the iris template that is of size [20 × 240] is split into four blocks and each of the blocks is of size [10 × 120]. The example of image splitting is shown in Figure 29. Then the upper left most iris image or block is used in the following steps. We only choose the left upper most because based on the observation on the iris template in the pre-processing phase it shows that most of the features are located in the upper block and the lower block only contains the eyelids and the pupil. Besides that, by using this technique the size of the iris image is reduced and it can save a lot of space in the database.

• **PSO for feature extraction**

PSO algorithm has been used in searching the best crypt in the iris template. This situation has the dimensions of fitness value, meaning that the PSO has a searching space with one dimension where the x-axis represents velocity of the particle and the y-axis represents position of the particle. The particular situation was chosen because both criteria could optimise or identify best crypt in the iris template. Particles attempt to move in the search space in order to find the best fitness function.

The implementation of finding crypts is done using the PSO approach which has been categorised into three modules. All modules are arranged according to the PSO process. In this research, MATLAB has been used as the main platform in developing the proposed method.

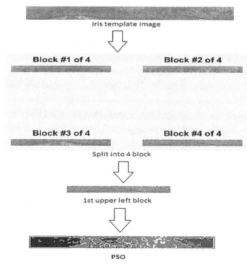

Figure 29: Split Block Process.

• **Bi-Cubic Interpolation**

Bi-cubic interpolation is a technique that interpolates a small 2D crypt image into a new crypt image size. The iris template is either successfully or not successfully matched in the matching process since it is totally dependent on the pixel values of a point at p(x,y) on a grid surrounding the crypt using methods such as the nearest-neighbour and interpolating them to approximate the values of its surrounding points. To smooth the positions of the crypts on the iris template, the crypt image is resampled with a few number of artefacts.

• **Matching**

The last phase is the matching phase. In this phase hamming distance is used as the technique to compare the crypt image. The Hamming distance algorithm employed also incorporates noise masking, so that only significant bits are used in calculating the Hamming distance between two iris templates. Now when taking the Hamming distance, only those bits in the iris pattern that correspond to '0' bits in noise masks of both iris patterns is used in the calculation. The Hamming distance is calculated using only the bits generated from the true iris region, and this modified Hamming distance formula is given as

$$HD = \frac{1}{N - \Sigma_{k=1}^{N} Xn_k (OR) Yn_k} \sum_{j=1}^{N} X_j (XOR) Y_j (AND) Xn_j^1 (AND) Yn_j^1$$

Where Xj and Yj are the two bit-wise templates to compare, Xnj and Ynj are the corresponding noise masks for Xj and Yj, and N is the number of bits represented by each template. Although, in theory, two iris templates generated from the same iris will have a Hamming Distance of 0.0, in practice this will not occur.

From the calculated Hamming distance values, only the lowest is taken, since this corresponds to the best match between two templates. The example code of Hamming distance is provided as:

```
hd=hammingdist(temp, temp2);
set(handles.hmi, `Visible`,`on`);
set(handles.hmi2, `Visible`,`on`);
set(handles.hmi, `String`, hd);
  if (hd<=0.25)
    set(handles.match, `Visible`, `on`);
    set(handles.notmatch, `Visible`, `off`);
  else
    set(handles.match, `Visible`, `off`);
    set(handles.nomatch, `Visible`, `on`);
  end;
```

Hamming Distance of Inter-Class Image

Inter-class similarity refers to how a biometric trait can be very similar for different persons. Inter-class similarity is exemplified in which two iris images of a pair of identical twins are shown. The two iris images are from different persons different classes) but since they are identical twins, their iris appearance is extremely similar. Moreover, several instances of distance between input image and all images in the database are considered. There are fifty classes, in which each class consisted of ten versions that were written as 001L01, 001L02, 002L01, ..., 050R01. The highlighted data meant that the data belonged to the same class as the input image, and contributed to the genuine distribution. Besides that, data that were not highlighted are data from different classes and make a contribution to non-genuine distributions.

Results from several distance values between input iris images and the images in the database were sorted from the closest to the furthest. Four samples of input images, namely user 001L01, 011L06, 029R10 and 006R01 were evaluated and contained only fourteen closest distances. The outcome shows a good matching result, in which seven iris images were identified as genuine from a total of eight images that represent one individual (class). At this point, it may be said that the matching rate is nearly achieved.

However, a poor matching result is expected since the images belongs to a particular class and did not have the closest distance to the input image of the corresponding class. All the images from the same class were ranked from number one to fourteen, but not at the highest ranks. The worst condition was only five from the same class obtained the smallest distance. The distance values expose inter-class variability.

5.3.4 Hamming Distance of Intra-Class Image

Intra-class variability refers to how a biometric trait can appear very different in multiple acquisitions of the same individual. Intra-class variability is exemplified, in which two different impressions of the same iris from the same subject are highlighted. Although the two images are impressions of the same iris of the same person (same class), the second impression contains a large amount of distortion compared to the first one. The matching rank and Hamming distance from the images in one class are measured. The intra-class of user 028 was represented and the matching rate approached 100%. For inter-class of user 028, the matching rate varied in the range of 25% to 75%. The distance values indicated that the intra-class variability was sufficiently high.

5.3.5 FAR and FRR Value

The overall performance of the proposed algorithm was assessed using FAR and FRR curves. The genuine distribution was generated from 938 genuine attempts. The has been observed that the intersection of non-genuine distribution and genuine distribution curves occurred at a threshold of 0.28. This point is called the Equal Error Rate (EER) point. From this EER point, the FAR value of 78.17% was obtained (that is the percentage of non-genuine occurrences at values less than 0.28), and the FRR value was 21.83% (that is the percentage of genuine occurrence at values higher than 0.28). The values of FRR and FAR describe the trade-off between security and the ease of the proposed algorithm. The low value of FAR shows that the system was considerably secure because the possibility that the system receives the iris image from an unregistered individual was small. Based on the data acquired from the simulation, from 262 non-genuine users trying to access system less than one individual was successful. On the other hand, high FRR values show that the system was very selective, and there was no guarantee that the registered user was accepted by the system.

The performance of PSO shows the EER value is 0.38 higher than the PSOBCI that indicates that the error rate of PSOBCI is lower compared to PSO as shown in Figure 30. It has proven that by combining the PSO with other techniques helps to reduce error rate of high noise environment of the iris template image.

The EER illustrates that the PSOBCI method was reduced to 0.28, which was lower than the PSO and Daugman methods that each gave

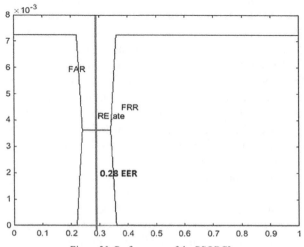

Figure 30: Performance of the PSOBCI.

0.38 and 0.3 EER values. This outcome signifies that the iris recognition system using PSOBCI manages to operate with lower error rates and detects the iris features better. Meanwhile, the EER of ACO is 0.25 and EACO is 0.21. A standard evaluation of Hamming Distance is between 0.3 to 0.5 HD.

5.4 DISCUSSIONS

Crypts are observed to be darker than their surroundings. Based on the 'contrast method' from the image retrieval field, the crypts pixel value is observed to be in the range of 30-to-90-pixels. The artificial ants have the capability of finding the same pixel values for crypts. The iris features are in grayscale format are in the range of 0 to 255 values. The '0' value means that the pixel value represents black while '255' represents white. The values between of '0' and '255' have the range of greyish to white. The radial furrow is brighter in colour compared to crypts for which the value is 120 to 160.

The artificial ants are released randomly for the first time to search for the crypts. They lay their pheromones as forward selection. The Ant Colony Optimization pheromone table of optimum solutions is updated to find iris features. The best-first self-searching method is implemented for finding the most converged.

During the matching process, the ant index image value is measured using Hamming Distance to find the similarity. When a perfect match is found, it gives the results as genuine. If there is no match for similarity in iris features, then the system informs a fake user (impostor). To determine a genuine user, the Hamming Distance (HD) is between zero 0.00 to 0.35 and "Match" appears on the screen to indicate that the matching process is successful. Meanwhile, if the Hamming Distance is more than 0.35 to 0.5, it declares the user as fake and a "Non-Match" alert is provided.

Moreover, the ant colony optimization approach gives a new perspective on the extraction phase, since this approach extracts among the best features of crypts and compares them based on the indexed crypt in the database. The new approach has been designed towards innovation in reducing error rates in the matching process and thus, provides better detection of iris features in iris recognition.

The first major findings are that, the matching process in the proposed approach has reduced the Equal Error Rate (EER) to 0.21 of the Hamming distance rate using the ant indexed features compared to 0.34 of the HD rate, which is based on non-indexed image matching. These findings add a significant addition to the body of knowledge in iris recognition, where, the new proposed approach can provide a better performance despite the fact that the iris features contain a considerable amount of distortion, noise and occlusion.

The later findings were that the performance accuracy of the enhanced ant colony optimization produced on average 76% to 85% accuracy, which did not achieve much improvement compared to previous methods (which achieved up to 99.99%). However, the findings also show that the values of precision performance obtained from this work have shown a significantly high improvement, which are in between 96% to 100%. Taken together, these results suggest that, despite the contradicting findings in accuracy and precision performances, the key strength of this study has shown that the use of blobs of iris features was capable of providing improvement in the iris recognition system. In particular, the new and novel approach shows that the iris recognition system is more resilient to errors caused by iris distortion. As a consequence, the iris system is capable of correctly identifying genuine users for a longer duration of time despite the fact that the users' irises are constantly changing due to aging, disease, growth, health conditions and emotions.

Subsequently, several beneficial contributions have been made to the biometric society by using the proposed enhanced ant colony optimization approach compared to other existing methods. The new approach has been found to be more cost effective, easily maintained, robust in exploration of human-aided recognition and long-term stability in iris databases.

Findings illustrate the outcome of PSO application and the PSO enhancement. The PSO enhancement consists of a combination of PSO and Bi-Cubic interpolation in iris recognition. In the implementation of PSO enhancement, 249 subjects from CASIA database have been tested. The outcome demonstrated that swarm intelligence approach is more effective in finding iris features. However, after the second and third matching attempts, the swarm-based classifier shows a better recognition and the error rate is reduced.

This implementation investigates how performance recognition falls with varying quality of images and reduces the high value of EER. ERR in PSO is 0.38 and in PSOBCI is 0.28. Using a combination of PSO and Bi-Cubic Interpolation recognition methods and one data-set with different levels of noise to evaluate the variations in the recognition error rates, produces an advantage in iris images with low noise levels and tends to contribute to a slight decrease in the recognition error rates of highly noisy iris images.

5.5 SUMMARY

The algorithm employs new covariance-based interpolation for edges and iterative curve-based interpolation for smooth areas. The results showed value has improved in terms of the quality of visual enhanced crypts images with the proposed method as compare to conventional methods.

PSO and ACO are currently two common techniques in swarm-inspired feature selection used to create iris templates in biometric recognition systems. PSO and ACO are both metaheuristic methods that have been widely used to solve different types of optimization problems. The main idea of ACO is to model the problem as the search for a minimum cost path in a graph using artificial ants. Each ant has a rather simple behavior so that it finds only poor-quality paths on its own. Better paths are found as the emergent result of the global cooperation among ants in the colony. This cooperation is performed in an indirect way through pheromone laying. Likewise, PSO is basically a population-based search procedure in which an individual particle adjusts its position according to its own experience, and the experience of the fittest neighboring particle. It optimizes a problem by iteratively trying to improve a candidate solution with regards to a given quality measure.

The implementation of ACO, EACO, PSO and PSOBCI in searching crypts in the iris template, involves the step-by-step explanation of all modules and has shown that the PSO algorithm has the capability to optimise the best crypt and ACO is able to search iris features even though the iris template is of low quality. The proposed models help us to understand and visualise the iris recognition process better in different perspectives. EACO and PSOBCI assist to accelerate the search elements to detect crypts and PSOBCI enlarges the crypt image for a faster matching phase.

CHAPTER 6

Conclusion

The legacy system of iris recognition has been designed to produce the IrisCode and established the iris recognition with the highest accuracy performance. However, as time goes on, the IrisCode, which is also called as iris template has been seen to constantly change due to factors of occlusion, pupil size variation, emotion, health condition, eye surgery, growth, and aging. On the other hand, the vulnerability points of the biometric system bring an opportunity for a hacker to attack the biometric system. Thus, a lot of techniques and methods have been developed in the first and second phases of iris recognition, to create innovations and finding solutions for a better iris recognition system. To improve the iris recognition system is through the use of swarm intelligence that offers an alternative approach from the legacy biometric system.

Therefore, the inspiration of swarm intelligence for iris recognition is designed to overcome problems that exist in the first and second phases of iris recognition. The swarm-based iris recognition has become one of the most important techniques for authenticating the identity of individuals. The analysis of the human iris is a reliable tool for authentication due to the blob of iris features. Iris features constitute one of the uniqueness, permanence, and performance biometric traits. Moreover, the iris is considered not easily tampered with biometric traits. The swarm-based iris recognition achieves a good accuracy performance and a lower rate of the equal error rate (EER) than the threshold value. A lower EER shows that the artificial insect tolerates noise from the iris image since the insect-based classifier finds blob inside the iris features using intelligent search and smart mechanisms.

In the swarm-based iris recognition, a genuine user is determined based on the individual characteristics of features such as crypt, pigment, and furrow in the human iris. It was found that the underlying foraging principle and the swarm optimization are integrated into evolutionary computational algorithms to provide a better search strategy for finding optimal feature vectors for iris recognition.

The artificial insect moves forward and backward in the same route. The iteration of movements in the same path is done until the searching process is converged. The parameter of precision is used to measure the convergence in the searching space. The best precision values determine the most accurate point. Accuracy is assumed to be high since the artificial insect makes a decision, which path to follow if a simultaneous searching point occurred. Moreover, it has addressed the common datasets of iris images analyzed for automatic iris recognition.

Based on the biometrics standard, that is ISO/IEC 2382-37:2012, the value of FAR is fixed at 0.1% using Hamming Distance as an indicator for verification performance. To determine a genuine, the Hamming Distance (HD) is between 0 to 0.3, and the "Match" result is to indicates that the matching process is successful. Meanwhile, if Hamming Distance shows the result is more than 0.3, it determines the user is not genuine and the result is "Non-Match".

The artificial insect performs a robust and intelligent search in finding the shape of crypt or furrow even though the quality of crypt image is in the high noise. The artificial insect locates the shape of the crypt in the low and high quality crypt by marking it with the artificial pheromone. A trail of movements or size and silhouette of the swarm indicate a convergence process and the significant points in the trail or silhouette need to be marked and stored in the database. To achieve a robust behaviour of the artificial classifier, a training process is implemented to make sure that the artificial classifier learns well and rapidly recognizes the crypt or furrow during the testing process, or called the matching process.

In the matching process, the point of similarities is compared between the stored iris template and the real-time iris template. The matching is going to be fast when the artificial classifier has identified the region-of-interest (ROI) during the training. The outcome of the matching produces in between 75% to 86% gives a significant result for iris recognition. Furthermore, the EER value indicates 0.2% to 0.22% from the standard value. Finally, the swarm intelligence for iris recognition provides cost-effective, rapid detection, robustness, and lightweight mechanisms for user authentication.

References

Abdul Matin, Mahmud Firoz, Zuhori Syed Tauhid and Sen, B. 2016. Human iris as a biometric for identity verification. pp. 1–4. *In*: 2nd International Conference on Electrical, Computer & Telecommunication Engineering (ICECTE).

Abikoye Oluwakem C., Adewole, J.S., Kayode, S. and Rasheed Jimoh. 2014. Iris feature extraction for personal identification using fast wavelet transform (FWT). International Journal of Applied Information Systems, 6(9): 1–6. ISSN 2249-0868.

Academy of Sciences Malaysia. 2017. Science and Technology Foresight Malaysia 2050, Emerging Science, Engineering & Technology (ESET) Study.

Adler, A. 2003. Sample images can be independently restored from face recognition templates. pp. 1163–1166. *In*: Proceedings of Canadian conference on Electrical and Computer Engineering.

Adler, A. 2005. Vulnerabilities in biometric encryption systems. pp. 211–228. *In*: Kanade, T., Jain, A. and Ratha Person. Authentication. LNCS. 3546, Springer, New York.

Adrian A. Lahola-Chomiak and Michael A. Walter. 2018. Molecular genetics of pigment dispersion syndrome and pigmentary glaucoma: New insights into mechanisms. Journal of Ophthalmology, Article ID, 5926906: 1–12.

Al-allaf, O.N.A. 2015. Improving the performance of particle swarm optimization for iris recognition system using independent component analysis. pp. 111–117. *In*: 2015 World Congress in Computer Science, Computer Engineering, and Applied Computing (WORLDCOMP'15) The 17th International Conference on Artificial IntelligenceAt: Nevada-Las Vegas-USA.

Alaoui, F. 2013. Application of blind deblurring algorithm for iris biometric. International Journal Computer Application, 79(3): 11–15.

Albert R. Wielgus. 2005. Melanin in human irises of different color and age of donors. Pigment Cell Research, 18(6): 454–464.

Ali, H.S., Ismail, A.I., Farag, F.A. and El-Samie, F.E.Abd. 2016. Speeded up robust features for efficient iris recognition. SIViP, 2016(10): 1385–1391.

Alice Nithya, A. and Lakshmi, C. 2017. Towards enhancing non-cooperative iris recognition using improved segmentation methodology for noisy images. Journal of Artificial Intelligence, 10(3): 76–84.

Alkoot M. Fuad. 2012. A review on advances in iris recognition methods. International Journal of Computer Engineering Research, 1–9.

Alonso-Fernandez, F., Tome-Gonzalez, P., Ruiz-Albacete, V. and Ortega-Garcia, J. 2009. Iris recognition based on SIFT features. *In*: 2009 1st IEEE International Conference on Biometrics, Identity and Security (BIdS).

Almisreb, A.A., Md Tahir, N., Ismail, A.I. and Abdullah, R. 2011. Enhancement pupil isolation method in iris recognition. pp. 1–4. *In*: Proceedings—2011 IEEE International Conference on System Engineering and Technology.

Amjed Noor, Khalid Fatimah, Rahmat et al., 2018. Noncircular iris segmentation based on weighted adaptive hough transform using smartphone database. Journal of Computational and Theoretical Nanoscience, 15(2): 739–743.

Andersen-Hoppe, E., Rathgeb, C. and Busch, C. 2017. Combining multiple iris texture feature for unconstrained recognition in visible wavelengths. pp. 1–6. *In*: 5th International Workshop on Biometrics and Forensics (IWBF). Article no. doi: 10.1109/IWBF.2017.7935090.

Arsalan, M., Naqvi, R.A., Kim Dong-Seop, Nguyen, P.H., Owais, M. et al. 2018. Iris dense net: robust iris segmentation using densely connected fully convolutional networks in the images by visible light and near-infrared light camera sensors. Sensors, 18(1501): 1–30.

Bachoo, A.K. and Tapamo, J.R. 2004. A segmentation method to improve iris based identification. pp. 403–408. *In*: 7th AFRICON IEEE Conference in Africa.

Baker, S., Bowyer, K.W. and Flynn, P.J. 2009. Empirical evidence for correct iris match score degradation with increased time-lapse between gallery and probe matches. *In*: Proc. Int. Conf. on Biometrics (ICB 2009).

Baker Ann-Marie, Gabbutt Calum, William, M., Cereser, B., Noor Jawad et al. 2019. Crypt fusion as a homeostatic mechanism in the human colon. BMJ Journal, 0: 1–8.

Bai, Q. 2010. Analysis of particle swarm optimization algorithm. Computer and Information Science, 3(1): 180–184.

Bender, E. 2015. Pigment Blotches. Available at http://bendereye.com/.

Bianco, C. 2015. How Vision Works. How Stuff Works Health [Online]. Available: http://health.howstuffworks.com/mental-health/human-nature/perception/eye1.htm.

Blum, C. and Dorigo, M. 2004. The hyper-cube framework for ant colony optimization. IEEE Transactions on Systems, Man, and Cybernetics—PART B: Cybernetics, 34(2). Available at: http://ai.unibo.it/system/files/u11/hypercube-ant.pdf.

Blum, C. 2005. Ant colony optimization: Introduction and recent trends. Physics of Life Reviees, 2(4): 353–373.

Boriev, Z., Nyrkov, A., Sokolov, S. and Chernyi, S. 2016. Software and hardware user authentication methods in the information and control systems based on biometrics. IOP Conference Series: Materials Science and Engineering, 124: 1–6.

Bowyer, K.W., Hollinsworth, K.P. and Flynn, P.J. 2007. Image understanding for iris biometrics: A survey. Computer Vision and Image Understanding, 110(2): 281–307.

Bowyer, K.W. and Ortiz, E. 2015. Iris recognition: does template ageing really exist? Biometric Technology Today, 10: 5–8.

Bramhananda Reddy, M.V. and Goutham, V. 2018. Iris technology: A review on iris based biometric systems for unique human identification. International Journal of Research-Granthaalayah, 6(1): 80–90.

Carneiro, M., Veiga, A., Castro, F., Flôres, E. and Carrijo, G. 2009. Processing the segmentation stage of an iris recognition system through evolutionary algorithm. Journal of Communication and Information Systems, 24. 10.14209/jcis.2009.2.

Castillo, O. and Melin, P. 2012. Optimization of type-2 fuzzy systems based on bio-inspired methods: A concise review. Information Sciences, 205: 1–19.

Chang, K., Bowyer, K.W., Sarkar, S. and Victor, B. 2003. Comparison and combination of ear and face images in appearance-based biometrics. IEEE Transactions on Pattern Analysis and Machine Intelligence, 25(9): 1160–1165.

Charlotte, A. Hall and Robert P. Chilcott. 2018. Eyeing up the future of the pupillary light reflexin neurodiagnostics. Dianostics MDPI, 8(19): 1–20.

Chen, Y., Adjouadi, M., Han, C., Wang, J., Barreto, A. et al. 2010. A highly accurate and computationally efficient approach for unconstrained iris segmentation. Image and Vision Computing, 28(2): 261–269.

Chen, Y., Yang, F. and Chen, H. 2013. An effective iris recognition system based on combined feature extraction and enhanced support vector machine classifier. Journal of Information and Computational Science, 10(60971089): 5505–5519.

Chen, Y., Liu, Y., Zhu, X., He, F., Wang, H. et al. 2014. Efficient iris recognition based on optimal subfeature selection and weighted subregion fusion. The Scientific World Journal, 2014: 157–173. doi: 10.1155/2014/157173.

Chen, Y., Liu, Y., Zhu, X., Chen, H., He, F. et al. 2014a. Novel approaches to improve iris recognition system performance based on local quality evaluation and feature fusion. The Scientific World Journal, 2014(6): 1–21.

Chen, H., Woodward, M.A., Burke, D.T., Jeganathan, V.S.E., Demirci, H. and Sick, V. 2017. Human iris three-dimensional imaging at micron resolution by a micro-plenoptic camera. Biomedical Optics Express, 8(10): 4514–4522.

Chu, C.-H.C. and Te, C. 2005. Fusion of Face and Iris Features for Multimodal Biometrics [online]. ICB 2006, LNCS 3832 © Springer-Verlag Berlin Heidelberg 2005. Available at: http://perso.telecom-paristech.fr/~chollet/Biblio/Articles/Domaines/BIOMET/Congres/ICB/2006/fq758532n13170vv.pdf.

Climent, J. and Hexsel, Roberto A. 2012. Iris recognition using AdaBoost and Levenshtein distances. International Journal of Pattern Recognition and Artificial Intelligence, 26(2): 1–20.

Clyde, W. Oyster. 1999. The Human Eye [online]. Sinauer Associates, Inc. Publishers Sunderland, Massachusetts. Available at: http://sinauerd.nextmp.net/media/wysiwyg/tocs/HumanEye.pdf.

Colorni, A. 1994. Ant system for job-shop scheduling. Belgian Journal of Operations Research, Statistics and Computer Science.

Connor, B.O. and Roy, K. 2014. Iris recognition using level set and local binary pattern. International Journal of Computer Theory and Engineering, 6(5): 416–420.

Czajka, A. 2013. Influence of iris template aging on recognition reliability. pp. 1–16. *In*: Communications in Computer and Information Science.

Daugman, J. 1993. High confidence visual recognition of persons test of statistical independence. IEEE Transactions on Pattern Analysis and Machine Intelligence, 15(11): 1148–1161.

Daugman, J. 1994. Biometric personal identification system based on iris analysis. US Patent, Patent Number 5291560, pp. 1–24.

Daugman, J. 2004. How iris recognition works. IEEE Transactions on Circuits and Systems for Video Technology, 14(1): 21–30.

Daugman, J. 2006. Probing the uniqueness and randomness of iriscodes: Results from 200 billion iris pair comparisons. Proceedings of the IEEE, 94(11): 1927–1934.

Daugman, J. 2007. New methods in iris recognition. IEEE Transactions on Systems, MAN and Cybernetics, 37(5): 1167–1175.

Daugman, J. 2015. Information theory and the IrisCode. IEEE Transactions on Information Forensics and Security, 11(2): 1–10.

Daugman, J. and Downing Cathryn. 2015. Searching for doppelgängers: assessing the universality of the IrisCode impostors distribution. IET Biometrics Journal, 1–11.

Daugman, J. 2016. Information theory and the IrisCode. IEEE Transactions on Information Forensics and Security, 11(2): 400–409.

Daugman, J. 2016. Iris image quality metrics with veto power and nonlinear importance tailoring. pp. 83–100. *In*: Rathgeb, C. and Busch, C. [eds.]. Iris and Periocular Biometric Recognition. IET Publishing. ISBN: 978-1-78561-168-1.

Daugman, J. Evolving Methods in Iris Recognition 200 Billion Iris Comparisons.

De Almeida, F.L. and Franca, R.N. 2017. Image quality treatment to improve iris biometric systems. INFOCOMP, 16(1-2): 21–30.

Dengwen, Z. 2010. An edge-directed bicubic interpolation algorithm. pp. 1186–1189. *In*: Proceedings—2010 3rd International Congress on Image and Signal Processing.

de Martin-Roche, D., Carmen Sánchez-Ávila and Raul Sánchez-Reillo. 1998. Iris recognition for biometric identification using dyadic wavelet transform zero-crossing. Semantic Scholar, 46(4): 1185–1188.

De Marsico, M., Nappi, M. and Riccio, D. 2012. Noisy iris recognition integrated scheme. Pattern Recognition Letters, 33(8): 1006–1011.

Devi, R., Uddin, J. and Hassan, Md. J. 2017. A new approach of iris detection and recognition. International Journal of Electrical and Computer Engineering, 7(5): 2530–2536.

Dgkrxg, D.K.G., Dqg, D., Plq, K., Jurzq, L.V., Rqh, D. et al. 2012. A new image segmentation method base on pso. The International Arab Journal of Information Technology, 9: 487–493.

Dong, W., Sun, Z. and Tan, T. 2009. A design of iris recognition system at a distance. pp. 1–5. *In*: Pattern Recognition, 2009. CCPR 2009. Chinese Conference.

Downing, J.D.C. 2001. Epigenetic randomness, complexity and singularity of human iris patterns [online]. Available at: http://rspb.royalsocietypublishing.org/content/royprsb/268/1477/1737.full.pdf.

Drozdowski, P., Garg, S., Rathgeb, C., Gomez-Barrero, M., Chang et al. 2018. Privacy-preserving indexing of iris-codes with cancelable bloom filter-based search structures. pp. 2374–2378. In European Signal Processing Conference (EURASIP).

Duncan Graham-Rowe. 2012. Ageing eyes hinder biometrics scans. Nature. doi: 10.1038/nature.2012.10722.

Dustin, Van Der Haar and Basie, Solms. 2014. The poor man's biometric: Identifying cost-effective biometric system criteria for SMME. pp. 1–10. *In*: Conference and Exhibition, IST-Africa.

Eberhart, R. and Kennedy, J. 1995. A new optimizer using particle swarm theory. A new optimizer using particle swarm theory. pp. 39–43. *In*: Proceedings of Sixth IEEE International Symposium on Micro Machine and Human Science.

Elizabeth Sidhartha, Monisha Esther Nongpiur, Carol Y. Cheung, Mingguang He, Tien Yin Wong et al. 2014. Relationship between iris surface features and angle width in Asian eyes. Investigative Ophthalmology & Visual Science, 55(12): 8144–8148.

Etin Indrayani. 2014. The Effectiveness and the efficiency of the use of biometric systems in supporting national database based on single ID Card Number (The Implementation of Electronik ID Card in Bandung). Journal of Information Technology & Software Engineering, 4(1): 1–9.

Fadi N. Sibai, Hafsa I. Hosani, Raja M. Naqbi, Salima Dhanhani and Shaikha Shehhi. 2011. Iris recognition using artificial neural networks. Expert Systems with Applications, 38: 5940–5946.

Fenker, S.P., Dame, N. and Bowyer, K.W. 2010. Experimental evidence of a template aging effect in iris biometrics. University of Notre Dame. pp. 232–239. IEEE Explore.

Fenker, S.P., Bowyer, K.W., Dame, N. and In, N.D. 2012. Analysis of template aging in iris biometrics. pp. 1–7. *In*: CVPRW.

Fenker, S.P., Ortiz, E. and Bowyer, K.W. 2013. Template aging phenomenon in iris recognition. IEEE Access, 1: 266–274.

Flom Leonard and Safir Aran. 1987. Iris recognition system. Patent Number US 4641349, 3 Feb 1987.

Flynn, P.J., Hall, F. and Dame, N. 2013. Are iris crypts useful in identity recognition? pp. 1–6. *In*: IEEE.

Forrester, J.V., Dick, A.D., McMenamin, P.G. and Roberts, F. 2008. The Eye: Basic Sciences in Practice, 3rd Edition. Saunders. Philadelphia, PA.

Gabriel, L.F.B.G., Azevedo, George D.C. Cavalcanti and Carvalho Filho, E.C.B. 2007. Hybrid solution for the feature selection in personal identification problems through keystroke dynamics [online]. Proceedings of International Joint Conference on Neural Networks, Orlando, Florida, USA, August 12–17. Available at: https://www.researchgate.net/profile/George_Cavalcanti/publication/224292722_Hybrid_Solution_for_the_Feature_Selection_in_Personal_Identification_Problems_through_Keystroke_Dynamics/links/00b49517e9e6c53fd4000000.pdf [Accessed 19 Jan 2016].

Garg, P. and Parashar, A. 2012. Feature selection method for iris recognition authentication system. Global Journal of Computer Science and Technology Graphics & Vision, 12(10): 28–32.

George W. Quinn, Patrick Grother and James Matey. 2019. pp. 1–37. *In*: IREX IX Part Two Multispectral Iris Recognition National institute of Standards and Technology (NIST).

Giachetti, A. and Asuni, N. 2008. Fast artifacts-free image interpolation. *In*: Proc. of the British Machine Vision Conforefence.

Gold, D.H. and Lewis, R.A. 2010. Clinical Eye Atlas. Oxford University Press.

Grosso, E., Pulina, L. and Tistarelli, M. 2012. Modeling biometric template update with Ant Colony Optimization. pp. 506–511. *In*: 5th IAPR International Conference Biometrics.

Guesmi, H., Trichili, H., Alimi, A.M. and Solaiman, B. 2012. Iris verification system based on curvelet transform. pp. 226–229. *In*: 2012 IEEE 11th International Conference on Cognitive Informatics and Cognitive Computing.

Gül, B.K. and Kurnaz, Ç. 2016. The impact of coding and noise on iris recognition system performance. pp. 1921–1924. *In*: 24th Signal Processing and Communication Application Conference (SIU), Zonguldak.

Guo, Q. and Zheng, J. 2018. An iris recognition algorithm for identity authentication. pp. 621–624. *In*: International Conference on Intelligent Transportation, Big Data & Smart City (ICITBS), Xiamen.

Habibah Adamu Biu, Rashid Husain and Abubakar S. Magaji. 2018. An enhanced iris recognition and authentication system using energy measure. Science World Journal, 13(1): 11–17.

Hala N. Fathee, Osman N. Ucan, Jassim M. Abdul-Jabbar and Oguz Bayat. 2019. Efficient unconstrained iris recognition system based on CCT-like mask filter bank. Hindawi Mathematical Problems in Engineering, 2019(Article ID 6575019): 1–10.

Han, F., Li, J., Qi, M. and Sheng, M. 2010. An approach of iris recognition based on partical swarm optimization. pp. 541–545. *In*: 2010 Fifth International Conference on Frontier of Computer Science and Technology.

Hande Husniye Telek, Hidayet Erdoi and Adem Turk. 2018. The effects of age on pupil diameter at different light amplitudes. Beyoglu Eye Journal, 3(2): 80–85.

Hanna, K., Mandelbaum, R., Mishra, D., Paragano, V. and Wixson, L. 1996. A system for non-intrusive human iris acquisition and identication. pp. 200–203. *In*: Proceedings of the International Association of Pattern Recognition Workshop on Machine Vision Applications, Tokyo, Japan, November 12–14.

Hao, F., Anderson, R. and Daugman, J. 2005. Combining cryptography with biometrics effectively. IEEE Trans. Comput., 55(640): 1081–1088.

Hassan, R., Kasim, S., Jafery, W.A. and Shah, Z.A. 2017. Image enhancement technique at different distance for iris recognition. International Journal on Advanced Science Engineering Information Technology, 7(4-2): 1510–1515.

Hashim, N., ZainalAbidin, Z. and Shibghatullah, A. 2016. A new model of crypt edge detection using PSO and Bi-cubic interpolation for iris recognition. pp. 659–669. *In:* Advanced Computer and Communication Engineering Technology. Springer.

He, F., Liu, Y., Zhu, X., Huang, C., Han, Y. et al. 2014. Multiple local feature representations and their fusion based on an SVR model for iris recognition using optimized Gabor filters. EURASIP Journal on Advances in Signal Processing, pp. 1–17.

Hezil, N., Hedjaz, H. and Abdelhani, B. 2015. Robust texture analysis approche for no-ideal iris recognition. pp. 1–5. *In:* 3rd International Conference on Signal, Image, Vision and their Applications.

Hollingsworth, K., Bowyer, K.W. and Flynn, P.J. 2007. All iris code bits are not created equal. pp. 1–6. *In:* IEEE Int. Conf. Biometrics Theory, Appl. Syst.

Hollingsworth, K., Bowyer, K.W. and Flynn, P.J. 2009. Image averaging for improved iris recognition. *In:* Proc. Int. Conf. on Biometrics (ICB 2009).

Hollingsworth, K., Bowyer, K.W. and Flynn, P.J. 2009. Pupil dilation degrades iris biometric performance. Computer Vision and Image Understanding, 113(1): 150–157.

Hsieh, L., Chen, W. and Li, T. 2010. Personal authentication using human iris recognition based on embedded zerotree wavelet coding. pp. 99–103. *In:* IEEE International Multi-Conference on Computing in the Global Information Technology.

Hudaib, A., Suleiman, D. and Awajan, A. 2016. A fast pattern matching algorithm using changing consecutive characters. Journal of Software Engineering and Applications, 9(8): 399–411.

Ives, R. and Matey, J. 2010. Design and implementation of a long range iris recognition system. pp. 1770–1773. *In:* Asilomar Conference on Signals, Systems and Computers (ASILOMAR).

Jagadeesh, N. and Patil, C.M. 2017. A brief review of the iris recognition systems for developing a user-friendly biometrie application. pp. 3309–3312. *In:* International Conference on Energy, Communication, Data Analytics and Soft Computing (ICECDS), Chennai, India.

Jain, A.K. and Ross, A. 2004. Multibiometric systems. Communications of the ACM, 47(1): 1–34.

Jamaludin, S., Zainal, N. and Zaki, W.M.D.W. 2018. Sub-iris technique for non-ideal iris recognition. Arabian Journal for Science and Engineering 43(12): 7219–7228.

June, C., Uma, K. and Geetha, P. 2011. Comparison of image compression using GA, ACO and PSO techniques. pp. 815–820. *In:* IEEE-International Conference on Recent Trends in Information Technology.

Kalavathi, P. and Bhonesh Narayani, J.M.R. 2016. IRIS segmentation using geodesic active contour method. Middle-East Journal of Scientific Research, 24(S2): 330–334.

Kanan, H.R., Faez, K. and Hosseinzadeh, M. 2007. Face recognition system using ant colony optimization-based selected features. pp. 57–62. *In:* IEEE Symposium on Computational Intelligence in Security and Defense Applications. Honolulu. doi: 10.1109/CISDA.2007.368135.

Kapoor, A., Caicedo, J.C., Lischinski, D. and Kang, S.B. 2014. Collaborative personalization of image enhancement. International Journal of Computer Vision, 108(1-2): 148–164.

Kapoor, P. and Rawat, P. 2017. Biometric quality: Analysis of iris recognition techniques with other biometric authentication systems. International Journal of Computer Application, 162(4): 31–36.

Kaur, B., Singh, S. and Kumar, J. 2018. Robust iris recognition using moment invariants. International Journal of Wireless Personal Communications, 99(2): 799–828.

Kaur, N. and Juneja, M. 2014. A review on Iris Recognition. 2014 Recent Advances in Engineering and Computational Sciences (RAECS), 2014: 6–8.

Kaur, S. and Garg, S. 2015. Analysis of iris recognition based on FAR and FRR using hough transform. IOSR Journal of Computer Engineering, 17(4): 31–36.

Khotimah, C. and Juniati, D. 2018. Iris recognition using feature extraction of box counting fractal dimension. Journal of Physics Conference Series, 947(2018): 1–6.

Khudher, I.M. and Ibrahim, Y.I. 2020. Swarm intelligent hyperdization biometric. Indonesian Journal of Electrical Engineering and Computer Science, 18(1): 385–395.

Kisku, D.R., Gupta, P., Sing, J.K. and Hwang, C.J. 2010. Multispectral palm image fusion for person authentication using ant colony optimization. pp. 1–7. *In*: 2010 International Workshop on Emerging Techniques and Challenges for Hand-Based Biometrics.

Ko, J.-G., Gil, Y.-H., Yoo, J.-H. and Chung, K.-I. 2007. A novel and efficient feature extraction method for iris recognition. ETRI Journal, 29(3): 399–401.

Kodituwakku, S. and Fazeen, M.I.M. 2008. An offline fuzzy based approach for iris recognition with enhanced feature detection. pp. 39–44. *In*: Advanced Techniques in Computing Sciences and Software Engineering. 10.1007/978-90-481-3660-5_7.

Kordsachia, C.C., Labuschagne, I. and Stout, J.C. 2018. Visual scanning of the eye region of human faces predicts emotion recognition performance in Huntington's disease. Neuropsychology, 32(3): 356–365.

Krichen, E., Allano, L., Garcia-Salicetti, S. and Dorizzi, B. 2005. Specific texture analysis for iris recognition. pp. 23–30. *In*: Int. Conf. on Audio- and Video-Based Biometric Person Authentication.

Kronfeld, P. 1962. Gross anatomy and embryology of the eye. H. Davison (edition). The Eye, Academic, London.

Lahola-Chomiak, A.A. and Walter, M.A. 2018. Molecular Genetics of pigment dispersion syndrome and pigmentary glaucoma: New insights into mechanisms. J Ophthalmol. doi: 10.1155/2018/5926906. PMID: 29780638; PMCID: PMC5892222.

Lee, C.-M. and Ko, C.-N. 2009. Time series prediction using RBF neural networks with a nonlinear time-varying evolution PSO algorithm. Neurocomputing, 73(1-3): 449–460.

Lee Eui Chul, Park Kang and Kim Jaihie. 2006. Fake iris detection by using Purkinje image. pp. 397–403. *In*: LNCS. 3832. 10.1007/11608288_53.

Liang, Y., Ding, X., Liu, C. and Xue, J.-H. 2016. Combining multiple biometric traits with an order-preserving score fusion algorithm. Neurocomputing, 171: 252–261.

Li, C., Xue, J., Quan, J., Yue, C. and Zhang, C. 2018. Biometric recognition via texture features of eye movement trajectories in a visual searching task. PLoS ONE. 13(4): e0194475. https://doi.org/10.1371/journal.pone.0194475.

Lim, K., Lee, K. and Kim, T. 2001. Efficient iris recognition through improvement of feature vector and classifier. ETRI Journal, 23(2): 61–70.

Linsangan Noel B., Panganiban Ayra G., Paulo R. Flores, Hazel Ann T. Poligratis, Angelo S. Victa et al. 2019. Real-time iris recognition system for non-ideal iris images. pp. 32–36. *In*: Proceedings of the 2019 11th International Conference on Computer and Automation Engineering.

Liu-jimenez, J., Member, S. and Sanchez-reillo, R. 2011. Iris biometrics for embedded systems. IEEE Transactions on Very Large Scale Integration (VLSI) Systems, 19(2): 274–282.

Liu, J., Fu, X. and Yao, X. 2012. PSO-RBFNN based optimized PNN classifier model. IEEE Transaction Computer Science and Network Technology, 456–459.

Liu, S., Liu, Y., Zhu, X. and Lin, Z. 2018. Ant colony mutation particle swarm optimization for secondary iris recognition. Journal of Computer-Aided Design and Computer Graphics, 30(9): 1604–1614.

Liu, X., Bowyer, K.W. and Flynn, P.J. 2005. Experiments with an improved iris segmentation algorithm. pp. 118–123. In: Proc. Fourth IEEE Workshop on Automatic Identification Technologies.

Li Yung-Hui and Huang Po-Jen. 2017. An accurate and efficient user authentication mechanism on smart glasses based on iris recognition. Mobile Information Systems, Article ID 1281020: 1–14.

Li Yung-Hui, Huang Po-Jen and Juan Yun. 2019. An efficient and robust iris segmentation algorithm using deep learning. Hindawi Mobile Information Systems, Article ID 4568929: 1–14. (http://biometrics.idealtest.org/).

Ma, L., Wang, Y. and Tan, T. 2002. Iris recognition based on multichannel gabor filtering. pp. 1–5. In: Proceedings of the 5th Asian Conference on Computer Vision. Melbourne, Australia.

Ma, L., Tan, T., Wang, Y. and Zhang, D. 2004. Efficient iris recognition by characterizing key local variations. IEEE Transactions on Image Processing, 13: 739–750.

Ma, L., Wang, K. and Zhang, D. 2009. A universal texture segmentation and representation scheme based on ant colony optimization for iris image processing. Comput. Math. with Appl., 57(11-12): 1862–1868.

Machala, L., Tichavsky, P. and Pospi, J. 2004. Human eye iris recognition using the mutual information. Optik, 115(9): 399–404.

Mahlouji, M. and Noruzi, A. 2012. Human iris segmentation for iris recognition in unconstrained environments. 9(1): 149–155.

Mancino, R., Di Carlo, E., Napoli, E., Martucci, A., Mauro, A. et al. 2018. Anterior segment optical coherence tomography analysis of iris morphometric changes induced by prostaglandin analogues treatment in patients with primary open angle glaucoma or ocular hypertension. Ophthalmology Journal, 12: 110–120.

Manjani, I., Sumerkan, H., Flynn, P.J. and Bowyer, K.W. 2016. Template aging in 3D and 2D face recognition. pp. 1–8. In: IEEE 8th International Conference on Biometrics Theory, Applications and Systems (BTAS).

Masek, L. 2003. Recognition of Human Iris Patterns for Biometric Identification. The University of Western Australia.

Matey, J.R., Broussard, R. and Kennell, L. 2010. Iris image segmentation and sub-optimal images. Image and Vision Computing, 28(2): 215–222.

Matey, J., Naroditsky, R.O., Hanna, K., Kolczynski, R., Lolacono, D.J., Mangru, S., Tinker, M., Zappia, T.M. and Zhao, W.Y. 2006. Iris on the MoveTM: Acquisition of images for iris recognition in less constrained environments. Proceedings of the IEEE 94(11): 1936–1946.

Matey, J.R., Tabassi, E., Quinn, G.W. and Chumakov, M. 2013. IREX VI temporal stability of iris recognition. Accuracy NIST Interagency Report 7948.

Mehrotra, H., Sa, P.K. and Majhi, B. 2013. Fast segmentation and adaptive SURF descriptor for iris recognition. Mathematical and Computer Modelling, 58(1-2): 132–146.

Melissa Edwards, David Cha, S. Krithika, Monique Johnson and Esteban J. Parra. 2015. Analysis of iris surface features in populations of diverse ancestry. Royal Society Open Science, 3(150424): 1–17.

Militello, C., Conti, V., Vitabile, S. and Sorbello, F. 2009. An embedded module for iris micro-characteristics extraction. pp. 223–230. In: International Conference on Complex, Intelligent and Software Intensive Systems.

Min, T.-H. and Park, R.-H. 2009. Eyelid and eyelash detection method in the normalized iris image using the parabolic Hough model and Otsu's thresholding method. Pattern Recognition Letters, 30(12): 1138–1143.

Minakshi Boruah. 2018. Evaluation of the parameters involved in the iris recognition system. Journal Advanced Computer Engineering Technology, 4(4): 219–228.

Min Beom Lee, Hyung Gil Hong and Kang Ryoung Park. 2017. Noisy ocular recognition based on three convolutional neural networks. Sensors, 17(2933): 1–26.

McDaniel, N. 2015. Freckles in iris features. Unitree Foundation Rayid International. [Online]. Available: http://rayid.com/main/structures.asp).

Michael G. Lorenz, Luis Mengibar Pozo, Judith Liu-Jimenez and Belen Fernandez-Saavedra. 2008. User-friendly biometric camera for speeding iris recognition systems. pp. 241–246. *In*: Proc of the 42th Annual IEEE International Carnahan Conferences Security Technology.

Mingyang Wang, Ningli Wang, Xiaorong Li and Guanglu Wang. 2018. A distinct form of retinitis pigmentosa with retinal vascular occlusion. International Journal of Clinical and Experimental Medicine, 11(6): 5802–5810.

Mithuna, K.T., Sasirekha, K. and Thangavel, K. 2017. Metaheuristic optimization algorithms based feature selection for fingerprint image classification. Proceedings of the International Conference on Intelligent Computing Systems (ICICS 2017). Sona College of Technology, Salem, Tamilnadu, India, 130–139.

Miyazawa, K., Ito, K., Aoki, T., Kobayashi, K. and Nakajima, H. 2005. A phase-based iris recognition algorithm. pp. 356–365. Advances in Biometrics, Springer Berlin/Heidelberg.

Mohsen Jenadeleh, Marius Pedersen and Dietmar Saupe. 2020. Blind quality assessment of iris images acquired in visible light for biometric recognition. Sensor, 20(1308): 1–22.

Monro, D.M., Rakshit, S. and Zhang, D. 2007. DCT-based iris recognition. IEEE Transactions on Pattern Analysis and Machine Intelligence, 29(4): 586–95.

Muroň, A. and Pospišil, J. 2000. The human iris structure and its usages. Physica, 39: 87–95.

Mustafa al Rifaee, Mohammad Abdallah and Basem Okosh. 2017. A short survey for iris images databases. Journal of Multimedia and its applications and Institute of Automation, 9(2): 1–14.

Neda Ahmadi and Gholamreza Akbarizadeh. 2015. Iris recognition system based on canny and LoG edge detection methods. Journal of Soft Computing and Decision Support Systems, 2(4): 26–30.

Neelima Chintala, Ravi Krishna Reddy, D. and Nagaraju, M. 2017. A novel approach for detecting the iris crypts. International Journal of Engineering Resaerch and Development, 13(6): 1–12.

Nguyen Kien, Fookes Clinton, Jillela Raghavender, Sridharan Sridha and Ross Arun. 2017. Long range iris recognition: A survey. Pattern Recognition 72(2017): 123–143.

Norma Ramirez and Rosaura Montelongo. 2018. Digital image processing to support iridology as a diagnostic alternative: A review. Academia Journal of Scientific Research, 6(11): 446–454.

Oh, J., Lee, U. and Lee, K. 2019. Usability evaluation model for biometric system considering privacy concern based on MCDM model. Security and Communication Networks, 2019(article ID 8715264): 1–14.

Omaima Al-Allaf, Abdelfatah Aref Tamimi, Shahlla A. AbdAlKader. 2012. Artificial neural networks for iris recognition system: Comparisons between different models. Architectures and Algorithms, 2(10): 744–752.

Omran, S.S. and Al-Hilali, A.A. 2018. Comparative study between different rectangle iris templates. pp. 7–12. *In*: 2018 International Conference on Advanced Science and Engineering (ICOASE), Duhok.

Othman Nadia. 2016. Fusion techniques for iris recognition in degraded sequences. PhD Thesis, University Paris-Sacly, France.

Padmanabhan, V. and Prabakaran, Dr. M. 2014. Object color graph based color image classification using intensity distributional matrix. *In*: International Journal of Inventions in Computer Science and Engineering.

Parpinelli, R.S., Lopes, H.S. and Freitas, A. 2002. Data mining with an ant colony optimization algorithm. IEEE Transactions on Evolutionary Computation, 6: 321–332.

Park, K.R. and Kim, J. 2005. A real-time focusing algorithm for iris recognition camera. Institute of the Electrical and Electronic Engineers Transactions on Systems, Man, and Cybernetics, 35: 441–444.

Paul, A., Khan, T.Z., Podder, P., Ahmed, R., Rahman, M.M. et al. 2015. Iris image compression using wavelets transform coding. pp. 544–548. International Conference on Signal Processing and Integrated Networks.

Pavan Verkicharla, Ankit Mathur, Edward Mallen, James Pope and David Atchison, David. 2012. Eye shape and retinal shape, and their relation to peripheral refraction. Ophthalmic & physiological optics. Journal of the British College of Ophthalmic Opticians (Optometrists), 32: 184–99.

Phillips, P.J., Bowyer, K.W., Flynn, P.J., Liu, X. and Scruggs, W.T. 2005. The iris challenge evaluation. *In*: Proc. IEEE Int. Conf. on Biometrics: Theory, Applications, and Systems.

Phillips, P.J., Scruggs, W.T., O'Toole, A.J., Flynn, P.J., Bowyer, K.W. et al. 2006 and ICE 2006 large-scale results. Technical Report National Institute of Standards and Technology.

Phillips, P.J., Scruggs, T., Flynn, P.J., Bowyer, K.W., Beveridge, R. et al. 2009. Overview of the multiple biometric grand challenge. *In*: Proc. Int. Conf. on Biometrics (ICB 2009).

Prajapati, H. and Bodade, R. 2017. Noise removal for unconstrained iris recognition. pp. 1–5. *In*: International Conference on Information, Communication, Instrumentation and Control (ICICIC).

Perez, C., Aravena, C.M., Vallejos, J.I., Estevez, P. and Held, C.M. 2010. Face and iris localization using templates designed by particle swarm optimization. Pattern Recognition Letters, 31(9): 857–868.

Proenca, H. and Alexandre, L.A. 2005. UBIRIS: A noisy iris image database. Covilha, Portugal.

Proença, H. 2006. Noisy Iris Database. Universidade da Beira Interior. Available: www.ubi.pt/UBIRISversion1.

Proenca, H. 2006. Towards non-cooperative biometric iris recognition. Thesis. University of Beira Interior.

Proença, H., Alexandre, L.A., Informatics, D. and Interior, B. 2006. Iris recognition: Measuring feature's quality for the feature selection in unconstrained image capture environments. pp. 1–6. *In*: IEEE International Conference on Computational Intelligence for Homeland Security and Personal Safety.

Proença, H. and Alexandre, L. 2010. Iris recognition: Analysis of the error rates regarding the accuracy of the segmentation stage. Image and Vision Computing, 28(1): 202–206.

Poonguzhali, N. and Ezhilarasan, M. 2015. Identification based on iris geometric features. Journal of Applied Sciences, 15: 792–799.

Popescu-Bodorin, N. and Balas, V. 2010. AI challenges in iris recognition. processing tools for bath iris image database. Recent advances in automation & information.

pp. 116–121. *In*: Proc. WSEAS 11th Int. Conf. on Automation & Information (ICAI'10).

Rachida Tobji, Wu Di, Naeem Ayoub and Samia Haouassi. 2018. Efficient iris pattern recognition method by using adaptive hamming distance and 1D log-gabor filter. (IJACSA) International Journal of Advanced Computer Science and Applications, 9(11): 662–669.

Radu, P., Sirlantzis, K., Howells, G., Hoque, S. and Deravi, F. 2012. Image enhancement vs feature fusion in colour iris recognition. pp. 53–57. *In*: Proceedings—3rd International Conference on Emerging Security Technologies, EST.

Rahman, Md., Podder Prajoy and Parvez, A.H.M. and Khan Tanvir. 2018. Ramifications and diminution of image noise in iris recognition system. *In*: IEEE International Conference on Current Trends towards Converging Technologies.

Rahib H. Abiyev and Koray Altunkaya. 2008. Personal iris recognition using neural network. International Journal of Security and its Applications, 2(2): 41–50.

Ramya, M. and Krishnaveni, V. 2016. Performance of machine learning classifier technique for iris recognition. Middle-East Journal of Scientific Research. Special Issue on Innovations in Information, Embedded and Communication Systems, (24): 39–46.

Ramos Vitorino and Almeida Filipe. 2000. Artificial Ant Colonies in Digital Image Habitats—A Mass Behaviour Effect Study. Pattern Recognition.

Rankin, D.M., Scotney, B.W., Morrow, P.J. and Pierscionek, B.K. 2012. Iris recognition failure over time: The effects of texture. Pattern Recognition, 45(1): 145–150.

Rankin, D.M., Scotney, B.W., Morrow, P. J. and Pierscionek, B.K. 2013. Iris recognition—the need to recognise the iris as a dynamic biological system: Response to Daugman and Downing. Pattern Recognition, 46(2): 611–612.

Rapaka, S. and Kumar, P.R. 2018. Efficient approach for non-ideal iris segmentation using improved particle swarm optimisation-based multilevel thresholding and geodesic active contours. IET Image Processing, 12(10): 1721–1729.

Rathgeb, C., Uhl, A. and Wild, P. 2012. Iris segmentation methodologies. pp. 49–73. *In*: Iris Biometrics, Springer.

Rao, U.H. and Nayak, U. 2014. Physical security and biometrics. *In*: The InfoSec Handbook. A press, Berkeley, CA. https://doi.org/10.1007/978-1-4302-6383-8_14.

Rawate, K.R. and Tijare, P.A. 2017. Human identification using iris recognition. IJSRSET, 3(2): 578–584.

Ren, X. and Fox, L.B. 2012. RGB-(D) Scene Labeling: Features and Algorithms [online]. *In*: Computer Vision and Pattern Recognition (CVPR), 2012 IEEE Conference. IEEE. Available at: http://ais.informatik.uni-freiburg.de/teaching/ws12/seminar_robotperception/06_Ren_RGBDSceneLabeling.pdf.

Ring, S. and Bowyer, K.W. 2008. Detection of iris texture distortions by analyzing iris code matching results. *In*: Proc. IEEE Int. Conf. on Biometrics: Theory, Applications, and Systems.

Roberto Pineda and Tulika Chauhan. 2016. Phakic intraocular lenses and their special indications. Journal of Ophthalmic and Vision Research, 11(4): 422–428.

Ross, A. 2010. Iris recognition: The path forward. Computer, 43: 30–35.

Rui Zhang and Yan Zheng. 2019. A survey on biometric authentication: Toward secure and privacy-preserving identification. IEEE Access, 7: 5994–6009.

Sahu, J. and Yadav, S. 2016. Indian iris recognition system using ant colony optimization. International Journal for Innovative Research in Science and Technology, 3(1): 197–204.

Salima Nebti and Abdallah Boukerram. 2017. Swarm intelligence inspired classifiers for facial recognition. Swarm and Evolutionary Computation, 32: 150–166.

Samir Shah and Arun Ross. 2006. Generating synthetic irises by feature agglomeration. *In*: ICIP, Atlanta, USA. Available at: http://citeseerx.ist.psu.edu/viewdoc/download?doi=10.1.1.310.4185&rep=rep1&type=pdf.

Sanchez-Avila, C., Sanchez-Reillo, R. and de Martin-Roche, D. 2002. Iris-based biometric recognition using dyadic wavelet transform. IEEE Access, October: 3–6.

Sansola Alora. 2015. Postmortem iris recognition and its application in human identification. M.S. Thesis. Boston University, Boston, MA, USA.

Saranya Devi, A. and Annapoorani, B. 2016. Efficient iris image compression using curvelet transform. International Journal of Scientific Engineering and Applied Science, 2(5): 410–413.

Sarika B. Solanke and Ratnadeep R. Deshmukh. 2017. Enhanced feature extraction technique for iris template generation. International Journal of Computer Technology & Applications, 8(4): 499–506.

Shailesh Arrawatia, Priyanka Mitra and Brij Kishore. 2017. Critical literature survey on iris biometric recognition. International Journal of Scientific Research in Science and Technology, 3(6): 600–605.

Shaikh, N.F. 2013. Improving the accuracy of iris recognition system using neural network and particle swarm optimization. International Journal of Computer Applications, 79(3): 1–6.

Sharkas, M. 2016. A neural network based approach for iris recognition based on both eyes. pp. 253–258. *In*: SAI Computing Conference.

Shen, F. and Flynn, P.J. 2012. Iris matching by crypts and anti-crypts. pp. 208–213. *In* 2012 IEEE Conference on Technologies for Homeland Security.

Shen, F. and Flynn, Patrick J. 2014. A visually interpretable iris recognition system with crypt features. PhD Thesis, Program in Computer Science and Engineering, University of Notre Dame, Indiana, USA.

Sheng-Hsun Hsieh, Yung-Hui Li, Wei Wang and Chung-Hao Tien. 2018. A novel anti-spoofing solution for iris recognition toward cosmetic contact lens attack using spectral ICA analysis. Sensors, 18(795): 1–15.

Silva Teodoro, F.G., Peres, S.M. and Lima, C.A.M. 2017. Feature selection for biometric recognition based on electrocardiogram signals. pp. 2911–2920. *In*: International Joint Conference on Neural Networks.

Singla, S.K. and Sethi, P. 2012. Challenges at different stages of an iris based biometric system. Songklanakarin Journal of Science and Technology, 34(2): 189–194.

Sivakamasundari, J., Devi Lakshmi, A., Madhumitha, P. and Pallabi Ghosh. 2019. Application of harmony search algorithm in retinal biometric system. Indian Journal of Public Health Research and Development, 10(7): 1779–1783.

Subha, S. and Devi, L. 2019. Iris biometric system and the challenges—A review. IOSR Journal of Engineering (IOSR JEN), 39–43. ISSN(e): 2250–3021, ISSN(p): 2278–8719.

Sun, S.N. and Zhao, L.D. 2012. Bovine iris segmentation using region-based active contour model. Int. J. Innov. Comput. Inf. Control., 8(9): 6461–6471.

Sun, Z., Wang, Y., Tan, T. and Cui, J. 2005. Imroving iris recognition accuracy via cascaded classifiers. IEEE Trans. Syst. MAN Cybern. 35(3): 435–441.

Sturm, R.A. and Larsson, M. 2009. Genetics of human iris colour and patterns. Pigment Cell Melanoma Res., 22(5): 544–62. doi: 10.1111/j.1755-148X.2009.00606.x. Epub 2009 Jul 8. PMID: 19619260.

Swihura, A. 2013. Pupil Zone Contraction. Saint Francis University. Available: https://www.studyblue.com/#flashcard/view/15380528.

Tajouri, I., Aydi, W., Ghorbel, A. and Masmoudi, N. 2017. Efficient iris texture analysis method based on Gabor Ordinal measures. Journal of Electronic Imaging, 26(4): 43012.

Tan, T. 2010. Biometrics Ideal Test Website. National Laboratory of Pattern Recognition (NLPR) and Institute of Automation, Chinese Academy of Sciences (CASIA).

Tan, T., Zhang, X., Sun, Z. and Zhang, H. 2012. Noisy iris image matching by using multiple cues. Pattern Recognition Letters, 33(8): 970–977.

Tiwari, U., Kelkar, D. and Tiwari, A. 2012. IRIS recognition based on PCA based dimensionality reduction and SVM. Int. J. Comput. Appl., 49(3): 28–32.

Tobji, R., Di, W., Ayoub, N. and Haouassi, S. 2018. Efficient iris pattern recognition method by using adaptive hamming distance and 1D Log-Gabor Filter. International Journal of Advanced Computer Science and Applications, 9(11): 662–669.

Toli Christina-Angeliki and Prencel Bart. 2018. Privacy-preserving biometric authentication model for e-finance application. pp. 353–345. *In*: International Conference on Information Systems Security and Privacy.

Trokielewicz, M. 2015. Linear regression analysis of template aging in iris biometrics. pp. 1–6. *In*: IEEE IWBF.

Trokielewicz, M., Czajka, A. and Maciejewicz, P. 2017. Iris recognition under biologically troublesome conditions—effects of aging, diseases and post-mortem. pp. 1–6. *In*: Conference of BIOSIGNALS.

Trokielewicz, M., Czajka, A. and Maciejewicz, P. 2018. Cataract influence on iris recognition performance. 929020-1-929020-14. *In*: Proceedings of SPIE.

Trokielewicz, M., Czajka, A. and Maciejewicz, P. 2015. Assessment of iris recognition reliability for eyes affected by ocular pathologies. pp. 1–6. *In*: 7th IEEE International Conference on Biometrics: Theory, Applications and Systems (BTAS 2015) At: Arlington, VA, USA.

Trujillo, L., Olague, G., Hammoud, R. and Hernandez, B. 2005. Automatic feature localization in thermal images for facial expression recognition. *In*: Proceedings of the 2005 IEEE Computer Society Conference on Computer Vision and Pattern Recognition (CVPR'05)—Workshops, San Diego, CA, USA, 1–14.

Tsai, C., Lin, H., Taur, J. and Tao, C. 2012. Iris recognition using possibilistic fuzzy matching on local features. IEEE Transactions on Systems, Man, and Cybernetics, Part B (Cybernetics), 42(1): 150–162. doi: 10.1109/TSMCB.2011.2163817.

Umer, S., Dhara, B.C. and Chanda, B. 2015. Iris recognition using multiscale morphologic features. Pattern Recognit. Letter., 65: 67–74.

Urashveen Kour, Satnam Singh Dub and Bhanu Gupta. 2019. Performance evaluation of iris recognition system using genetic, algorithm optimization. International Journal of Scientific Research and Engineering Development, 2(1): 86–92. ISSN: 2581-7175.

Venkatesan, S. and Srinivasa Rao Madane. 2010. Face recognition system with genetic algorithm and ANT colony optimization. International Journal of Innovation, Management and Technology 1(5): 469–471. ISSN: 2010-0248.

Vineet Kumar, Abhijit R. Asati and Anu Gupta. 2015. Iris localization based on integro-differential operator for unconstrained infrared iris images. pp. 277–281. *In*: International Conference on Signal Processing, Computing and Control (ISPCC).

Wang, J. 2018. An improved iris recognition algorithm based on hybrid feature and ELM. IOP Conference of Materials Science and Engineering, 322: 1–5.

Wang, Z., Dillon, J. and Gaillard, E.R. 2006. Antioxidant properties of melanin in retinal pigment epithelial cells. Photochemical Photobiology, 82: 474–479.

Wayman, J. 1999. Error rate equations for the general biometric system. Robotics. Automation Magazine, IEEE.

Wildes, R. 1997. Iris recognition: An emerging biometric technology, 85(9): 1348–1363. *In*: Proceedings IEEE.

Ye, L., Yang, M., Xu, L., Zhuang, X., Dong, Z. et al. 2014. Nonlinearity analysis and parameters optimization for an inductive angle sensor. Sensors (Basel, Switzerland), 14(3): 4111–25.

Zainal Abidin, Z., Manaf, M., Shibhgatullah Mohd Yunos, S.H.A., Anawar, S. et al. 2012. Iris segmentation analysis using integro-differential operator and hough transform in biometric system. J. Telecommun. Electron. Comput. Eng. 4(2): 41–48.

Zainal Abidin, Z., Manaf, M. and Shibhgatullah, A.S. 2013. Experimental approach on thresholding using reverse biorthogonal wavelet decomposition for eye image. pp. 349–353. *In*: IEEE International Conference on Signal and Image Processing Applications.

Zainal Abidin, Z., Manaf, M. and Shibhgatullah, A.S. 2014. Ant-CBIR: A new method for radial furrow extraction in iris biometric. pp. 20–25. *In*: International Conference on Information Security and Cyber Forensics.

Zainal Abidin, Z., Abal Abas, Z., Ahmad, R., Hashim, N.A. and Ramli, M.R. 2017. Crypt matching using EACO for iris recognition. International Journal of Applied Engineering Research, 12(22): 12814–12820.

Zhang, X., Xiong, Q. and Xu, X. 2018. Iris identification app based on andriod system. In Proceedings of the 2018 Chinese Automation Congress (CAC), Xi'an, China, 2229–2234.

Zhang, H., Liu, J., Zeng, Z., Zhou, Q., Li, S. et al. 2018. Hybrid fusion framework for iris recognition systems. *In*: 13th Chinese Conference, Proceedings on CCBR. Urumqi, China. doi: 10.1007/978-3-319-97909-0_50.

Zhao, D., Luo, W., Liu, R. and Yue, L. 2018. Negative iris recognition. pp. 112–125. *In*: IEEE Transactions on Dependable and Secure Computing, 15(1): 112–125.

Zhou, S.K. and Chellappa, R. 2006. Face recognition from multiple still images or a video sequence. pp. 547–567. *In*: Zhao, W. and Chellappa, R. [eds.]. Face Processing: Advanced Modeling and Methods, Elsevier.

Zhu, X., Li, N. and Pan,Y. 2019. Optimization Performance comparison of three different group intelligence algorithms on a svm for hyperspectral imagery classification. Remote Sensing MDPI, 11(734): 1–20.

Zeitz, C., Scheidat, T., Dittman, J. and Vielhauer, C. 2008. Security issues of internet-based biometric authentication systems: risks of man-in-the-middle and Biophishing on the example of BioWebAuth. pp. 68190R.1–12. *In*: Delp, E., Wong, P., Dittmann, J. and Memon, N. [eds.]. Security, Forensics, Steganography and Watermarking of Multimedia Content. Proceedings of SPIE. 6819. SPIE, Bellingham, WA.

Index